SCHOLASTIC

Using Picture Books to Teach 8 Essential Literary Elements

Susan Van Zile, Mary Napoli
& Emily Ritholz

- Setting
- Point of View
- Plot
- Characterization
- Theme
- Foreshadowing
- Flashback
- Figurative Language

New York • Toronto • London • Auckland • Sydney
Mexico City • New Delhi • Hong Kong • Buenos Aires

Teaching Resources

Edited by Mela Ottaiano
Cover design by Jorge J. Namerow
Interior design by Melinda Belter
Interior illustrations by Melinda Belter and Brian LaRossa

ISBN: 978-0-545-33518-8

Printed in the U.S.A.

1 2 3 4 5 6 7 8 9 10 40 18 17 16 15 14 13 12

CONTENTS

INTRODUCTION

Like yours, our classrooms are filled with high-quality literature to share with our students. Upon entering our classrooms, you will find books in baskets, on shelves, and most important of all, in the hands of our students. As Judith Langer's (2011) research indicates, "Literature allows students to explore possibilities and consider options while gaining connectedness and vision of their world and thinking" (page 2). Outstanding selections of literature provide students with opportunities to encounter diverse voices and cultures, while offering multiple examples of text structures, devices, and literary elements.

With increased emphasis on addressing the Common Core State Standards for English Language Arts, teachers face the challenge of guiding students to understand that literary elements and devices play a key role in helping them comprehend and communicate a story's meaning. Our goal is for students to read beyond the words and literal meaning in order to be swept up by the multiple inferences that shape and extend their thinking.

We also want to invite students to consider how writers use language, symbolism, and other literary devices to foreshadow events and determine outcomes. Authors use literary devices to make their writing more vivid and memorable; without these devices, writing can be lifeless and dull (Lukens, 2006). In Hall's (2002) work about using picture books to teach literary devices, she explains that students need to understand, interpret, and apply their growing knowledge of literary devices in their own literary repertoire. Recognizing and understanding various literary devices is only one component of being able to read and write critically. Literary devices are employed by authors to make their words more expressive. For instance, a writer would use devices such as metaphor or simile to enhance his or her work. As students learn to recognize literary devices, interpret them, and explain why and how an author uses them, they can infuse these in their own writing (Olness, 2005). In contrast, literary elements are the components or building blocks of a whole piece of writing. Good readers and writers not only examine the book's overall effect on the reader, but also the elements that produce this effect. By exploring and discussing traditional literary elements of setting, characterization, theme, point of view, and so on with readers, you will enhance their ability to evaluate and select quality literature.

High-quality picture books are exemplary models of language that provide readers with multiple opportunities to make meaning, learn the techniques good writers use in their writing, and explore literary elements. In Smith & Wilhelm's (2010) book, *Fresh Takes on Teaching Literary Elements*, the authors emphasize the importance of actively engaging with texts to make meaning while exploring literary elements. Their research about literacy has guided our understanding of how we can help our students transfer what they learn from reading one text to their reading of other texts (page 11). Teaching students strategies to unlock literary analysis by identifying literary devices and investigating the effects of those devices makes it possible to promote the reading and inferential skills students need to construct their own interpretations (Vásquez, 2009).

In the following pages, we have applied the theoretical underpinnings of the latest literacy research to help you and your students navigate literature in purposeful ways. As we extend our initial exploration of using picture books to teach literary elements (Van Zile & Napoli, 2009), we present more than 100 book annotations, organized by literary element: setting, point of view, plot, characterization,

Literary Elements

SETTING

POINT OF VIEW

PLOT

CHARACTERIZATION

THEME

FORESHADOWING

FLASHBACK

FIGURATIVE LANGUAGE

We want our students to read beyond the words and literal meaning and to be swept away in the inferences that drive their thinking. Exposing students to high-quality texts in a variety of genres provides them with multiple levels of meaning. This annotated bibliography includes more than 100 outstanding selections of literature along with easy-to-implement lessons and activities.

theme, foreshadowing, flashback, and figurative language. In each annotation, we explain why it is a good model for teaching the element, and include a teaching idea followed by an interdisciplinary reading or writing connection. There are also 16 focused lessons, two per literary element. Each lesson features a critical question, a list of necessary materials, and steps to guide students' understanding. In some cases, there is a student reproducible to help you explicitly teach the element. As a whole, the annotations provide you with many resources to guide students' literary understanding and transfer of literary elements.

FINDING PICTURE BOOKS

Picture books are an outstanding resource for reading aloud with students. Since the picture book format can be found in a variety of genres—historical fiction, realistic fiction, poetry, fantasy, and so on—it lends itself well to all learners. As Serafini (2009) notes, "the lyrical writing and exceptional artwork used in contemporary picture books anchors the sounds of written language in students, provides appropriate and enjoyable literary experiences and entices readers to interact with literature in a relatively 'risk-free' format." Kane (2008) and Moss (2005) consider picture books models of effective sentence structure, punctuation, word choice, voice, dialogue, figurative language, and so on.

As you can see by the Web Resources (at right), there are many different award lists that include excellent picture books for students and teachers. We recommend referring to these lists on a regular basis to access titles that will help students make reading and writing connections and obtain a deeper understanding of literary elements.

WEB RESOURCES *

The following websites provide information about award-winning books that may be used to teach literary elements.

- The American Library Association honors illustrators and authors with numerous awards, including the Caldecott, Coretta Scott King, Pura Belpré, and Robert Sibert awards. Visit www.ala.org for more information.
- The Children's Africana Book Awards were established in 1991 by the Outreach Council of the African Studies Association to encourage the publication and use of accurate, balanced children's books on Africa. The awards focus specifically on books published in the United States about Africa. Since 1991, 37 awards have been presented to the authors and illustrators of outstanding books. Awards are presented in two categories: Best Book for Young Children and the Best Book for Older Readers. Visit www.africaaccessreview.org/aar/awards.html for more information.
- The Children's Literature Assembly of the National Council of Teachers of English advocates the importance of utilizing literature for teaching children and young adults. Information about the Notable Children's Books in the Language Arts can be found at www.childrensliteratureassembly.org/.
- The Lee Bennett Hopkins Poetry Award is given to the best book of children's poetry published in the United States in the preceding year. Cosponsored with Mr. Hopkins, the University Libraries, and the Pennsylvania Center for the Book. Information can be found at www.pabook.libraries.psu.edu/activities/hopkins/hopkins.html.
- The Notable Books for a Global Society (NBGS) Committee, part of the International Reading Association Children's Literature and Reading Special Interest Group, annually selects a list of outstanding trade books for enhancing student understanding of people and cultures throughout the world. Winning titles include fiction, nonfiction, and poetry written for students in grades K–12. The winning titles each year are announced at the International Reading Association Convention. More information can be found at www.clrsig.org.
- The Notable Books for Teaching Social Studies (NCSS) list features books written primarily for children in grades K–8. The books align with the NCSS standards and emphasize a broad range of cultural experiences. Visit www.socialstudies.org/resources/notable for more information.

* **Note:** Throughout this book, there are listings for websites that you or your students might find helpful. At the time this book went to press, the website addresses were correct. Before students access any site, please preview it to be sure the material is suitable for their developmental level and academic needs.

CONNECTIONS TO THE COMMON CORE STATE STANDARDS

The activities and lessons in this book will help you meet your specific state reading and language arts standards as well as those recommended in the Common Core State Standards (CCSS). Listed below are the specific CCSS Reading Standards for Literature (RL) addressed in each section. For more information about the CCSS, visit www.corestandards.org.

SETTING	**Key Ideas and Details** RL.4.3: Describe in depth a character, setting, or event in a story or drama, drawing on specific details in the text (e.g., a character's thoughts, words, or actions). RL.7.3: Analyze how particular elements of a story or drama interact (e.g., how setting shapes the characters or plot). RL.8.2: Determine a theme or central idea of a text and analyze its development over the course of the text, including its relationship to the characters, setting, and plot.
POINT OF VIEW	**Craft and Structure** RL.4.6: Compare and contrast the point of view from which different stories are narrated, including the difference between first- and third-person narrations. RL.5.6: Describe how a narrator's or speaker's point of view influences how events are described. RL.6.6: Explain how an author develops the point of view of the narrator or speaker in a text. RL.7.6: Analyze how an author develops and contrasts the points of view of different characters or narrators in a text.
PLOT	**Key Ideas and Details** RL.4.3: Describe in depth a character, setting, or event in a story or drama, drawing on specific details in the text (e.g., a character's thoughts, words, or actions). RL.5.3: Compare and contrast two or more characters, settings, or events in a story or drama, drawing on specific details in the text (e.g., how characters interact). RL.6.3: Describe how a particular story's or drama's plot unfolds in a series of episodes as well as how the characters respond or change as the plot moves toward a resolution. RL.7.3: Analyze how particular elements of a story or drama interact (e.g., how setting shapes the characters or plot). RL.8.3: Analyze how particular lines of dialogue or incidents in a story or drama propel the action, reveal aspects of a character, or provoke a decision.
CHARACTER-IZATION	**Key Ideas and Details** RL.4.3: Describe in depth a character, setting, or event in a story or drama, drawing on specific details in the text (e.g., a character's thoughts, words, or actions). RL.5.3: Compare and contrast two or more characters, settings, or events in a story or drama, drawing on specific details in the text (e.g., how characters interact). RL.6.3: Describe how a particular story's or drama's plot unfolds in a series of episodes as well as how the characters respond or change as the plot moves toward a resolution. RL.7.3: Analyze how particular elements of a story or drama interact (e.g., how setting shapes the characters or plot). RL.8.3: Analyze how particular lines of dialogue or incidents in a story or drama propel the action, reveal aspects of a character, or provoke a decision.

THEME	**Key Ideas and Details** RL.4.2: Determine a theme of a story, drama, or poem from details in the text. RL.5.2: Determine a theme of a story, drama, or poem from details in the text, including how characters in a story or drama respond to challenges. RL.6.2: Determine a theme or central idea of a text and how it is conveyed through particular details; provide a summary of the text distinct from personal opinions or judgments. RL.7.2: Determine a theme or central idea of a text and analyze its development over the course of the text; provide an objective summary of the text. RL.8.2: Determine a theme or central idea of a text and analyze its development over the course of the text, including its relationship to the characters, setting, and plot.
FORE-SHADOWING	**Craft and Structure** RL.5.5: Explain how a series of chapters, scenes, or stanzas fits together to provide the overall structure of a particular story, drama, or poem. RL.6.5: Analyze how a particular sentence, chapter, scene, or stanza fits into the overall structure of a text and contributes to the development of a theme, setting, or plot.
FLASHBACK	**Craft and Structure** RL.5.5: Explain how a series of chapters, scenes, or stanzas fits together to provide the overall structure of a particular story, drama, or poem. RL.6.5: Analyze how a particular sentence, chapter, scene, or stanza fits into the overall structure of a text and contributes to the development of a theme, setting, or plot.
FIGURATIVE LANGUAGE	**Craft and Structure** RL.5.4: Determine the meaning of words and phrases as they are used in a text, including figurative language such as metaphors and similes. RL.6.4: Determine the meaning of words and phrases as they are used in a text, including figurative and connotative meanings; analyze the impact of specific word choice on meaning and tone. RL.7.4: Determine the meaning of words and phrases as they are used in a text, including figurative and connotative meanings; analyze the impact of rhymes and other repetitions of sounds (e.g., alliteration) on specific verse or stanza of a poem or section of a story or drama. RL.8.4: Determine the meaning of words and phrases as they are used in a text, including figurative and connotative meanings; analyze the impact of specific word choices on meaning and tone, including analogies or allusions to other texts.

CHAPTER 1 • SETTING

> ***"The days grow shorter, but there is still no darkness. The sun just hides a little longer below the northern horizon. Sunset colors linger until the sun rises again and follows a circular path around the top of the spinning world."***
>
> —from *Arctic Lights, Arctic Nights* (page 6) *

The setting of a story, poem, or play is the time and place of the action. Elements of setting include specific geographic locations; seasons; time of day or more general references to the past, present, or future; historical eras; and culture. Descriptions of the setting engage the reader by creating a vivid mental picture of the characters' location in space and time. In addition, the imagery and details also create an atmosphere or mood that frequently elicits an emotional response in the reader. Like other literary elements, setting "facilitates the understanding of characters and their actions" (Roberts, 2009), the plot, and the theme.

Implicit in both the definition and example of setting are the following characteristics:

- a physical description of place
- a time
- a social/emotional dimension that influences the characters and their relationships
- mood and atmosphere

To guide students' understanding and analysis of setting and in order for the transfer between reading and writing to occur in their own work, it is important to teach the characteristics of setting in an explicit manner.

LESSON 1

Changes in Setting—The Truth Revealed

MODEL TEXT

Letting Swift River Go
Written by Jane Yolen
Illustrated by Barbara Cooney
Little, Brown, 1992, 32 pp.

Letting Swift River Go is a bittersweet story of the creation of the Quabbin Reservoir, located in central Massachusetts, between 1927 and 1946. Yolen employs a poetic narration of Sally's voice as she recollects the realities of living near the flooding of the swift-river towns and the disappointment of leaving the tranquil rural community. Sally's family is forced to move, rowing along the reservoir to safety. As Sally remembers her childhood, she

MATERIALS

- 1 copy of *Letting Swift River Go*
- crayons, markers, colored pencils
- plain white paper
- 1 copy of Swift River Valley Time Line (page 17), cut into cards
- large sheet of butcher paper divided into ten numbered sections
- tape
- sentence strips

* **Note:** Many of the picture books in this resource are unpaginated. Page numbers are given to assist you in locating text and are based on standard pagination.

remembers with fondness her town before the flood. She recalls as well, with sadness, the dismantling of the town, its history and identity—forcing families and friends to relocate. The luminous illustrations evoke a sense of time and place. The double-page spreads of pictorial vignettes will help readers visualize the devastation of a town and to empathize with those who lost their homes. The last scene illustrates the narrator (Sally) and her father revisiting the reservoir, pointing out underwater landmarks, and finally looking "down into the darkening deep and letting them go," referring to the collective memories of their beloved town.

CRITICAL QUESTION

How do changes in setting reveal a truth?

WARM-UP

After distributing sheets of plain white paper to students, invite them to draw a picture of a simple landscape. Afterward, have students exchange their pictures with a partner. Direct students to draw an object that makes a simple change to the landscape. Have students share the changes they made and name one positive and one negative effect the change has had on the environment.

STEP BY STEP

1. Read aloud *Letting Swift River Go*. Ask students, as they listen to the story, to think about man's effect on the environment. Engage in a discussion of students' observations after reading.
2. Hand out one Swift River Valley Time Line card per student pair. Divide a large piece of butcher paper into ten numbered sections and tape it to the floor or wall.
3. Tell students to go to the section of butcher paper that matches the number on their card. Provide time for students to use crayons and markers to create illustrations that portray the meaning of the text on their card.
4. After students complete their drawings, have them tape their cards below the illustration. When the mural is complete, ask students to view it silently and to think about what the changes in the setting reveal.

VARIATION: As an alternative to the class mural, provide each pair of students with a piece of construction paper to illustrate. Then, hang the illustrations around the room in numerical order and have students do a gallery tour of the Swift River Valley Time Line.

WRAP-UP

On a sentence strip, have students write a single sentence that states a "truth" about man's impact on the environment as depicted in the mural. To share, form a circle and call on each student to read his or her truth aloud.

LESSON 2

Creating Atmosphere in Writing

MODEL TEXT

The Cats in Krasinski Square
Written by Karen Hesse
Illustrated by Wendy Watson
Scholastic, 2004, 32 pp.

Based on a true story that took place in the Warsaw Ghetto during the Nazi occupation, this is a powerful portrayal of a young Jewish girl who, together with her older sister, displays courage and hope during a bleak historical era. Karen Hesse's clear free verse introduces readers to the protagonist, a young

MATERIALS

- 1 copy of *The Cats in Krasinski Square*
- copies of the Drawing Frame activity (page 18; 1 copy per student pair)
- crayons, markers, colored pencils
- copies of Word Clouds (page 19; 1 copy per student)

Jewish girl, and her sister, who bring food to the people in the ghettos. The opposition movement orchestrates a plan to transport food by train to reach hungry Jews living behind the walls. However, the Nazi soldiers learn about the scheme and wait at the train station with dogs. The many cats that surround the square inspire a solution. The young protagonist, her sister, and other Resistance fighters gather up the cats in Krasinski Square and take them to the train station. They release the cats, distracting the dogs and creating pandemonium. The brave people were able to smuggle the food to the ghetto without being caught.

CRITICAL QUESTION

What is atmosphere, and why is it important to develop atmosphere in my writing?

ATMOSPHERE: The overall emotional feeling created by the details the author uses; atmosphere is created through descriptions of settings, characters, and events.

WARM-UP

Pair students and allow partners to decide who will be the author and who will be the illustrator. Distribute the reproducible Drawing Frame activity to each pair. Tell students that they will have five minutes to complete this activity. The student playing the author will respond verbally to the prompt on the reproducible, creating the atmosphere for the illustrator. The illustrator will create the atmosphere being described. Once complete, students should hold up the images. Sharing visual images demonstrates that there are infinite possible atmospheres for every sentence. The key is how you express yourself.

STEP BY STEP

Karen Hesse uses repetition, descriptive language, and her unique voice to create atmosphere in *The Cats in Krasinski Square*. Wendy Watson, illustrator of the book, uses a palate that adds hope and uplifted spirits to a dark and fearful time.

1. Pass out to students the Word Clouds reproducible.
2. Read aloud the picture book *The Cats in Krasinski Square*. Ask students to think about the words and phrases that lend atmosphere to the story and to jot them down in the clouds on their graphic organizer.
3. Provide an opportunity for students to share thoughts with a partner about the words and the illustrations.
4. Invite students to make connections to the themes of helping others and rising above personal fears.

WRAP-UP

Ask partners to come up with an alternate setting that could also be described by the words on their handouts and to be ready to share that setting with the class.

More Books for Teaching SETTING

Arctic Lights, Arctic Nights

Written by Debbie S. Miller
Illustrated by Jon Van Zile
Walker & Company, 2003, 32 pp.

In this visually stunning, nonfiction picture book, the author presents vivid descriptions about arctic animals and weather throughout the changing seasons. The author, a resident of Fairbanks, Alaska, chronicles the seasonal changes that take place throughout the Alaskan wilderness. On every page, readers will learn a wealth of information about this natural phenomenon. Readers will be captivated by the author's rich use of language that describes the sights, sounds, and feel of the Arctic as the year progresses. The end pages provide a detailed glossary to include in a writer's notebook or science journal.

TEACHING IDEA

■ Ask students to pay close attention to the illustrations on each page. With a partner, they should then describe the uniqueness of color and light to depict the way animals and nature adapt to the seasonal changes.

INTERDISCIPLINARY CONNECTIONS

■ Encourage students to keep track of and record times for sunrise and sunset, as well as the average high/low temperatures on the twenty-first of each month. Invite them to create models to examine the relationship that the earth and sun have on seasonal change and the length of the day.

■ Discuss the seasons and the changes in the length of the days of each month as seen in the book. Ask: *How does the change in the seasons relate to the length of day? Are seasonal changes noticeable? How do seasonal changes affect the plants and animals? How would seasonal changes affect humans?*

Coming on Home Soon

Written by Jacqueline Woodson
Illustrated by E. B. Lewis
G. P. Putnam's Sons, 2004, 32 pp.

Ada Ruth tries her best to be brave when her mother decides to go to Chicago to work on the railroads during World War II. Due to the difficult economic times, Ada Ruth remains at home with her grandmother. Ada Ruth knows her mother loves her more than rain and more than snow, but she still misses her more and more. She waits impatiently for a letter from her mother. A homeless kitten that appears on their doorstep helps to keep Ada Ruth and her grandmother company as they patiently wait for communication from Ada Ruth's mother. When a letter finally arrives, there is a promise that her mother will be coming home soon. The illustrations in the book are full of light, echoing the hope and longing of Grandmother and Ada Ruth. The light and shadowing in the illustrations, coupled with the emotional text, serve as the springboard for an exploration of setting. Sometimes the light in the illustrations shines through the window, or streams of light appear in an open door.

TEACHING IDEA

■ Students can write a letter from Ada Ruth's mother describing what it is like working far from home and family. Encourage students to use descriptive elements about Ada Ruth's mother's surroundings, emotions, and routines.

INTERDISCIPLINARY CONNECTIONS

■ Students can compare and contrast life in Ada Ruth's small town community to life in the city of Chicago.

■ Read and discuss other books about women going to work during World War II.

Crow Call

Written by Lois Lowry
Illustrated by Bagram Ibatoulline
Scholastic, 2009, 32 pp.

Poignant and powerful, this story demonstrates the effect of war on family relationships. When Lizzie's father returns from World War II, she feels like he is a complete stranger, a man who doesn't even know her favorite food is cherry pie. As the two set out on an early morning journey to hunt crows, Lizzie, dressed in her coveted too-long wool shirt, receives a crow call from her father. Afraid of her dad, who is a hunter, Lizzie subtly expresses her desire to simply call, not kill, the crows. While Lizzie's dad explains the need to shoot the crop-eating crows, he never fires his gun and delights in the sheer joy and power Lizzie experiences as she calls the crows. Timeless and universal, the theme of this story—a parent and child yearning to understand one another—is conveyed in both the rich sensory language and stunning illustrations that capture the deep emotional bonds forged between the characters in the midst of the austere fall setting.

TEACHING IDEA

■ Invite students to consider the setting and its appeal to the five senses. Guide them to record language that provides a clear image of the setting and discuss the relationships between the setting and the experiences of the main character(s).

INTERDISCIPLINARY CONNECTION

- Ask students to select a historical event that the class is exploring and complete a "historical figure" journal entry based on the experiences of the individual. Encourage students to write details about the period and setting to help readers visualize its time, place, and mood.

Dandelions

Written by Eve Bunting
Illustrated by Greg Shed
Harcourt, 1995, 48 pp.

In this historical-fiction picture book, Zoe and her family move from Illinois to Nebraska. Everyone is excited about their new sod house, new neighbors, and new town. Zoe's mama, on the other hand, is nostalgic for her old friends. So, on a day trip to town with her father, Zoe notices a mass of dandelions growing in the prairie and decides to surprise her mother by replanting them to her room. Her mother says, "Don't expect a miracle, Zoe. It will take time," which is representative of Mama's own feelings of becoming acclimated to her new environment. The very last spread shows a roof crowned in dandelion gold. The messages of survival, strength, pride, courage, and love are depicted through the beautiful language and illustrations.

TEACHING IDEAS

- In this story, the dandelions symbolize the beauty found in simple things as well as the love for others. Invite students to find a piece of music, a painting, or a poem that visually represents a feeling evoked by the dandelions.
- The story contains many metaphors to make the writing more interesting. Ask students to identify the metaphors related to mood and atmosphere. For example, just like Zoe's family, the dandelions are not easily transplanted, but they eventually take root and become part of the new landscape of home.

INTERDISCIPLINARY CONNECTIONS

- Read and discuss other books that are set in the mid- to late 1800s. Discuss how during this period, people from all over the eastern part of the United States were migrating out west to find better lives for themselves and their families. Use a T-chart to compare and contrast the experiences of Zoe's life with that of your students' lives.
- Have students use a Five Senses graphic organizer to identify the five senses described in the book. Ask students to work in pairs to complete the graphic organizer and to share their descriptions of what the scene or character being described looks like, sounds like, tastes like, smells like, and feels like. Then have students use this organizer as a guide to write and illustrate a sensory poem.

Freedom Summer

Written by Deborah Wiles
Illustrated by Jerome Lagarrigue
Atheneum Books for Young Readers, 2001, 32 pp.

Set in the 1960s, this historical-fiction picture book shares the story of two best friends, John Henry and Joe. The boys spend the summer days doing a lot of things together, but when they learn that they can't swim in the town pool because it is for white people only, they resolve to go to the local creek. However, the narrator of the story, Joe, who is white, learns that the law has changed to allow everyone to use the town pool. Throughout the story, readers will learn about the pain and injustice of segregation. The atmospheric paintings coupled with the poetic language make the story even more poignant.

TEACHING IDEA

- The author's style includes many statements to establish setting. Invite readers to listen for those descriptions as the action moves to different locations (e.g., description of the action at Fiddlers Creek, the empty pool, or the country store). Record the different statements on chart paper and encourage students to borrow this style when writing their own stories. For example, "It is so quiet now, we can hear the breeze whisper through the grass. We sit on the diving board and stare at the tops of the silver ladders sticking up from the tar."

INTERDISCIPLINARY CONNECTIONS

- Ask students to imagine that they are either Joe or John Henry and write about their experience inside the country store as they went in together. Ask them to write from the perspective of the character.

- Conduct a Web quest to learn more about the civil rights movement.

The Girl on the High-Diving Horse

Written by Linda Oatman High
Illustrated by Ted Lewin
Philomel, 2003, 40 pp.

In this unique picture book, readers will meet Ivy Cordelia, the daughter of a photographer who makes a living on the boardwalk in Atlantic City. Set in the 1930s, the author and illustrator transport readers to the sights and sounds of strolling the boardwalk during the summer. Ivy is very excited to see the diving horses. What are diving horses? These trained horses, guided by a rider, dive from a high platform into a tank of water. Ivy has the chance to ride along with one of the professional riders on Red Lips, one of the high-diving horses. Ivy dreams of becoming one of the riders and ten years later, she returns to Atlantic City to become "the girl on the high-diving horse." The artwork and story fuse together, placing readers in the scene as if it were a photo snapshot. The author and illustrator add a personal note about their childhood memories and visits to the beach.

TEACHING IDEA

- Encourage students to listen for rich descriptions of setting that the author uses, including proper nouns and phrasing that appeals to the senses. Direct students to use a graphic organizer, such as the one found on page 19, to record and share these descriptions. Add the words they record to a sensory word wall for writing.

INTERDISCIPLINARY CONNECTIONS

- Provide disposable cameras to students to take snapshots of a favorite spot (hiking trail, backyard, lake, river, and so on). After developing photos, ask students to write sentences on index cards to describe the setting (what it looks like and the corresponding emotions of being in this place). Compile the photos and descriptions into a postcard book. If your school has digital cameras, students can also take turns using these.

- Invite students to write a personal narrative about an important event in their lives.

The Lotus Seed

Written by Sherry Garland
Illustrated by Tatsuro Kiuchi
Harcourt, 1993, 32 pp.

In this beautiful story about family heritage, a young girl takes a seed from a lotus pod to remember the emperor's abdication. She takes out this same lotus seed throughout her childhood, after she marries, and even when she has escaped her war-torn homeland. The treasured lotus seed serves as a reminder of her heritage, hope, and courage as she shares the story with her own grandchildren. The sparse but eloquent language, coupled with the beautiful illustrations, pays tribute to the powerful message that even a small object, like a seed, can hold vivid memories.

TEACHING IDEA

- Remind students that the lotus seed is a keepsake from the grandmother's immigration to the United States. She cherishes the seed and the memories the seed preserves for her about her heritage. Ask students to bring in family artifacts/treasures and share the meaning with others. Prompt students to use sensory language to describe one thing in their home that has special meaning to them or to their family. Ask students to draw and write about this item and invite the class to go on an "artifact/treasure walk" while considering how the descriptions evoked emotions and mood.

INTERDISCIPLINARY CONNECTIONS

- Use the Internet to take a visual tour of Vietnam and learn about various aspects of the culture. Discuss the multiple themes that stem from this story, such as courage, keeping traditions alive, emotional hardship, sadness, and sharing memories.

- Share information about the Statue of Liberty and what this symbol represents. The American Family Immigration History Center (AFIHC) at Ellis Island is an official site for the Statue of Liberty; there is information about 25 million immigrants, passengers, and crew members who entered New York Harbor between 1892 and 1924.

- Discuss immigration and launch an inquiry project about family history. Have students create a visual representation, such as a lotus flower, that they can use to document background information about their family.

Night of the Gargoyles

Written by Eve Bunting
Illustrated by David Wiesner
Clarion, 1994, 32 pp.

In this picture-book fantasy, an assortment of gargoyles comes alive to "creep on stubs of feet," along ledges and in dark rooms. In beautiful free verse, the eerie physical descriptions are precise (e.g,. their tongues "green pickled at the edges"). The gargoyles that adorn the walls of a museum come to life with Wiesner's duotone charcoal illustrations. He plays with light against dark, forming menacing shadows, and includes picture spreads with narrow and wide-angle views that create a deliciously, spooky scene. The gargoyle creatures hunch and grunt together at a spitting water fountain, complain about the weather, make unkind faces to the museum guard and then fly home. The line and texture of the illustrations help to create a distinct mood while also accentuating personified gargoyle creatures.

TEACHING IDEAS

- Ask students to look closely at the details of the carvings and drawings of the gargoyles. Then ask them to draw a gargoyle and to write a detailed description so that another person can replicate it without looking at their drawing. Discuss how the illustrations and language evoked an emotional response.
- Use the following review points to guide students as they examine the gargoyles and these characters' relationship to setting and mood.

CHARACTERS: Point out facial expressions, actions, and other interesting or supporting details.

SETTING: Go over the arrangement of each page, including the foreground and background.

MOOD: Ask students: *How does the author want the reader to feel?*

Then, have students work with a partner to discuss the facial expressions, actions, and other interesting details of the gargoyles to complete a four-column chart with the following headers:

PAGE #

FACIAL EXPRESSION

ACTION

INTERESTING DETAIL

Allow time for students to discuss how the illustrator has brought to life the gargoyles, the setting, and the mood.

INTERDISCIPLINARY CONNECTIONS

- Encourage students to learn more about the history of gargoyles. Gargoyles have combinations of natural, animal, and human qualities in their physical appearance. For example, they may have a human head covered with branches and leaves and a body like a lion. In the Middle Ages, gargoyles were carved from stone and displayed on towers and church entrances. Today, gargoyles can be seen on many churches in Europe and are popular as garden ornaments.
- Invite students to create a gargoyle sculpture out of clay and write a gargoyle (character) description about it. Ask them to use interesting details to describe the gargoyle's personality, where it lives, what kind of powers it has, what special features it has, and so on.

Owl Moon

Written by Jane Yolen
Illustrated by John Schoenherr
Philomel, 1987, 32 pp.

This classic story lovingly depicts the special relationship of a young child and her father as they take a nighttime stroll to look for owls. Through poetic and sensory language, readers will formulate vivid images and the sounds of a chilly winter evening. The illustrations evoke images of ice-covered branches, moonlit landscapes, and a winter night sky. The rich and evocative setting essentially becomes one of the characters.

TEACHING IDEAS

- Guide students to add sensory details to enhance the setting in their individual personal narratives. Use excerpts from the book to illustrate good examples of setting, such as "it was as quiet as a dream," and "our feet crunched over the crisp snow." Encourage students to visualize and discuss how the author's use of descriptive language helps them to connect the text and explore characters' interactions with the setting.
- Use the Sketch to Stretch strategy (Harste, Short, & Burke, 1988) to guide students to visualize the key ideas and details of the story. The strategy allows students to draw quick sketches to stretch their thinking and understanding of concepts. You can also use the strategy as a prewriting activity to help them sketch ideas that share details about a special place they would like to go to with someone important to them.

INTERDISCIPLINARY CONNECTIONS

- Use the book to spark inquiry about owls. Have students use the Internet, nonfiction books, and reference materials to learn more information about owls.
- Encourage students to revisit one of their personal narratives. Ask them to highlight the setting and work with a partner to add more sensory details.

Pappy's Handkerchief: A Tale of the Oklahoma Land Run

Written by Devin Scillian
Illustrated by Chris Ellison
Sleeping Bear Press, 2007, 40 pp.

This historical-fiction picture book shares the story of Moses, a young African-American boy, and his family's journey from their home in Baltimore to the Oklahoma territory. After a series of hardships, Moses is left to travel onward on his own, claiming the land by burying his father's handkerchief in the ground. The emotional impact of the story, its characters, and its historic setting is reinforced through the language and illustrations.

TEACHING IDEA

- Invite students to pay close attention to the details describing the journey Moses and his family took from Baltimore to the new land in the Oklahoma Territory. Ask students to use visual and literal clues to describe how Moses felt at the beginning, middle, and end of the story.

INTERDISCIPLINARY CONNECTIONS

- Read and discuss other books describing the hardships that families faced during the late 1800s.
- Invite students to write a letter from Moses to his father describing the new land, the surroundings, and his hopes for a better life.

Queen of the Falls

Written and illustrated by Chris Van Allsburg
Houghton Mifflin, 2011, 40 pp.

In *Queen of the Falls*, readers will meet Annie Edson Taylor, a 63-year-old widow, who decides to go over Niagara Falls in a barrel. Her determination and courage makes her somewhat of a celebrity as the first woman to go over the falls, in 1901. She designs a strong barrel to withstand the force of the falling water and convinces a barrel maker to construct it. On the day she is scheduled to go over the falls, spectators breathlessly watch as the barrel rolls to the edge of the falls and then plunges downward into the water. Annie survives and only has a few minor bruises. She is dubbed the "Queen of the Falls" and tours the country talking about her amazing adventure. Through stunning language and illustrations, Chris Van Allsburg creates memorable scenes to capture Annie's journey.

TEACHING IDEA

- During reading, chart the descriptive language about the setting and about how it serves as another "character" in the story. Also, discuss how the setting frames Annie's growth and courage throughout her journey.

INTERDISCIPLINARY CONNECTIONS

- Conduct an illustrator study and notice the details in Van Allsburg's work.
- Read more information about courageous women throughout history who were known as daredevils. Write a story about one of these women that includes a descriptive setting.

Saturdays and Teacakes

Written by Lester Laminack
Illustrated by Chris Soentpiet
Peachtree, 2004, 32 pp.

In this beautifully illustrated picture book, the author writes about a young boy's Saturday visit with his grandmother. During their visit, they talk, eat tomato sandwiches, and make teacakes. The special love between a child and his grandmother is shared with grace and integrity that will spark memoir writing with students. Through impeccable illustrations and brilliant prose, this story celebrates the special times with loved ones.

TEACHING IDEA

- During reading, record how the author describes his childhood town. Encourage students to pay close attention to how the main character's emotional traits and memories are closely tied to the descriptions of the setting.

INTERDISCIPLINARY CONNECTIONS

- After reading aloud the story, ask students to make a list of their own memories. Then, invite them to create a Heart Map, a visual representation displaying memories and topics that students hold close to their heart. Ask them to focus on one of these memories to write their own memoir, paying close attention to the five senses as they describe the setting and other features of the memory.
- While eating teacakes, enjoy listening to the author read the story at www2.scholastic.com/browse/media.jsp?id=621.

SWIFT RIVER VALLEY TIME LINE

1. "Mama let me walk to school all alone along the winding black top . . ." (page 4)

2. "We played mumblety-peg in the graveyard and picnicked on Grandpa Will's stone . . ." (page 6)

3. "I slept out under the back yard maples with Nancy Vaughan . . . we'd see the fireflies winking on and off and on." (page 9)

4. "First we moved the graves . . ." (page 17)

5. "Then the governor sent his 'woodpeckers' to clear the scrub and brush, to cut down all the trees . . ." (page 19)

6. "Our houses came next. Some were bulldozed . . ." (page 20)

7. "Strangers came with their big machines, building tunnels and caissons . . ." (page 24)

8. "The waters rose . . . like unfriendly neighbors halfway up the sides of the hills . . ." (page 26)

9. "Little perch now owned those streets, and bass swam over the country roads . . ." (page 28)

10. "[Swift River Valley] Gone, all gone, under the waters." (page 30)

DRAWING FRAME

Name: ______________________________

Decide who will be the author and who will be the illustrator. The author has five minutes to tell the illustrator, in the most descriptive language possible, the atmosphere in which the house next to the road exists. The illustrator must take the author's words and create a sketch in the frame that provides a visual image of the atmosphere. Be as specific as possible in your description and illustration.

"Once, there was a house next to a road . . ."

WORD CLOUDS

Name: ____________________

Use this graphic organizer to record words and phrases that lend atmosphere to a story.

CHAPTER 2 • POINT OF VIEW

> ***"Dear Mrs. LaRue,***
> ***Were you really so upset about the chicken pie? You know, you might have discussed it with me. You could have said, "Ike, don't eat the chicken pie. I'm saving it for dinner." Would that have been so difficult? It would have prevented a lot of hard feelings."***
>
> —from *Dear Mrs. LaRue: Letters From Obedience School* (page 7)

Point of view is the perspective from which a story is told. For fiction, the three most common points of view are first person, third-person limited, and third-person omniscient. For nonfiction, third-person objective viewpoint is often used.

Examining various characters' viewpoints or perspectives of an event or issue in a story helps students to become critical readers. Not only will analyzing point of view assist students in understanding the story, but it will also enhance students' ability to consider and evaluate other people's perspectives in the real world.

LESSON 3

Two Different Points of View

MODEL TEXTS

Back of the Bus
Written by Aaron Reynolds
Illustrated by Floyd Cooper
Philomel/Penguin, 2010, 32 pp.

On a normal day in Montgomery, Alabama, a boy and his mother are riding a bus—in the back where they are supposed to sit. But as the bus becomes more crowded, angry looks are given to the boy, his mother, and Mrs. Rosa Parks, who remain seated. The combination of the text and illustrations used throughout the book inform the reader that the bus is moving through the town, reinforced by phrases such as "more people pilin' on" and "some folks get up and new ones sit down." The rich dialogue and descriptive language will appeal to the reader's senses; it is certainly easy to picture "worked-all-day eyes," and hear a "crinkled-up-somethin's-wrong voice." Told from the unique perspective of the young boy and accompanied by powerful illustrations, this is a memorable historical-fiction picture book.

MATERIALS

- 1 copy of *Back of the Bus*
- 1 copy of *Rosa's Bus: The Ride to Civil Rights*
- 1 copy of Point of View and the American Flag (page 27; transparency or scanned copy to project onto a screen)
- copies of the Point of View Reference Chart (page 28; 1 copy per student)
- copies of What's the Point of View? (page 29; 1 copy per student)
- copies of Two Viewpoints (page 30; 1 copy per student)
- chart paper

Rosa's Bus: The Ride to Civil Rights

Written by Jo S. Kittinger
Illustrated by Steven Walker
Calkins Creek/Boyds Mill Press, 2010, 40 pp.

In this beautifully illustrated book, the story of Rosa Parks's historic 1955 bus ride is told from a unique perspective. It is the bus itself that shares what happened on the day when Rosa Parks refuses to give her seat to a white man. The lyrical writing coupled with the prominent oil paintings evokes emotions of courage and determination. The end of the book contains an author's note complete with additional information about Bus #2857, which has been fully restored and refurbished to be part of the Henry Ford Museum.

CRITICAL QUESTION

How do two different points of view contribute to an understanding of a specific moment in history?

WARM-UP

Project onto a screen a copy of Point of View and the American Flag. Explain to students that you are going to read aloud two paragraphs about the American flag. Direct students to listen to the different perspectives each writer has of the flag.

Read the paragraphs aloud. Afterward, discuss the differences between the two perspectives. Ask students how both paragraphs contribute to their understanding of the American flag. Invite students to consider how their knowledge of the flag would change if only paragraph two were present. What would be missing?

STEP BY STEP

1. Explain to students that they are going to listen to two different stories that focus on the same moment in history: Rosa Parks's bus ride on December 1, 1955.
2. Tell students that identifying the point of view before listening to each version of the event will help them interpret each narrator's perception of the event.
3. Distribute to students the Point of View Reference Chart. Review the definitions and examples of point of view with them. Discuss some of the other stories they have read and ask them to identify the point of view.
4. Pair students. Distribute copies of What's the Point of View? Review the directions, provide time for students to complete the activity, and discuss their answers.
5. Before reading aloud *Back of the Bus*, remind students to focus on the first-person narrator's description of Mrs. Parks when she refuses to move to the back of the bus.
6. After reading aloud the story, explain that you will reread a few pages that focus on the narrator's description of the bus incident, so that students can carefully reflect on the description. Using a document camera, project a copy of pages 14 and 15 or hold the book open to these pages and reread them. Follow the same procedure for pages 16 and 17.
7. Afterward, pair students again and distribute copies of Two Viewpoints. Review the directions with them and provide time for partners to discuss and record their observations of the first-person narrator's perceptions of the incident.
8. Next, read *Rosa's Bus: The Ride to Civil Rights*, this time asking students to focus on the third-person objective narrator's description of the bus incident.
9. After the first reading, project a copy of page 10 onto the screen and reread it. Repeat this procedure for pages 22 and 25.
10. Instruct partners to discuss and record their observations of the third-person objective narrator's perception of the incident and to answer the question at the bottom of the reproducible.
11. As a class, engage in a discussion about the different perspectives of the bus incident and how both perspectives enhance students' understanding of this historic moment.

WRAP-UP

As a class, brainstorm a list of historical events. Record students' responses on chart paper. Then direct students to choose one of these moments in history and write about it from two different points of view. Afterward, pair students and have them share their writings. If desired, ask students to illustrate the historic event, then display their illustrations and writing.

LESSON 4

Point of View: A Different Perspective

MODEL TEXT

Sweet Tooth

Written by Margie Palatini
Illustrated by Jack Davis
Simon & Schuster, 2004, 40 pp.

This humorous story, full of wordplay and personification, introduces readers to Stewart, a young boy who has an obnoxious tooth. Stewart's tooth is SO demanding, leading him to give in to all of its demands. The tooth shouts, "I NEED A CANDY BAR. NOW-OW!" or other demands at inopportune times, such as at the movies or at a family wedding. Finally, Stewart retaliates and decides to eat healthy foods.

MATERIALS

- 1 copy of *Sweet Tooth*
- 1 copy of Point of View Improv (page 31), cut into cards
- basket or hat
- copies of the Model Script for Different Points of View (page 32; 1 copy per student)
- 1 copy of Scenes From *Sweet Tooth:* Different Points of View (page 33), cut into strips

CRITICAL QUESTION

How does analyzing characters' perspectives help the reader understand point of view?

WARM-UP

Tell students that they are going to have the opportunity to do some improvisational acting to demonstrate point of view. Copy the Point of View Improv reproducible and cut out the cards. Place them in a hat or basket and allow student volunteers to select one. Give students who are acting one minute to prepare their improvisations. Allow the student who correctly identifies the character to be the next one to select from the basket. Discuss how each actor's point of view toward an event revealed his or her identity.

STEP BY STEP

1. Explain to students that their improvisations illustrated an object's perspective of a situation. Similarly, in addition to who is telling the story, point of view also relates to how characters in a story perceive events. Tell students to keep this in mind as you read aloud *Sweet Tooth.*
2. Next, inform students that they will engage in an activity designed to help them analyze different characters' perspectives of a specific event in *Sweet Tooth.*
3. Distribute the model script. Assign roles to students and have them dramatically read the script aloud. Discuss how the new perspectives and points of view change the meaning of the event.
4. Form five groups of four. Distribute a Scenes From *Sweet Tooth* scene strip to each group. Students may decide who will play each character.
5. After students brainstorm ideas for the scene, have them begin writing the script. Instruct each student to write down what the group decides, so that everyone in the group has his or her own copy of the script. Make sure a copy of *Sweet Tooth* is available so that students can review the scenes they have been assigned.
6. Suggest that each character in the skit be responsible for creating his or her lines. Stress that throughout the writing process the group must convey each person's point of view.
7. Provide time to practice and perform the skits.

WRAP-UP

After each performance, compare and contrast the events portrayed and note the similarities and differences between the skits and the actual story.

Ask students why they think the author chose to omit some of the perspectives students dramatized from the story. How do the various perspectives change the reader's understanding of the story?

More Books for Teaching POINT OF VIEW

Dear Mrs. LaRue: Letters From Obedience School

Written and illustrated by Mark Teague
Scholastic, 2002, 32 pp.

When Mrs. LaRue becomes frustrated by her dog's antics, she sends Ike to obedience school. From the "prison," known as Brotweiler Canine Academy, Ike writes letters to Mrs. LaRue detailing the horrors to which he is subjected. The illustrations, however, tell a very different story. Ike writes postcards to his owner to persuade her to release him early. When she refuses, Ike is forced to escape on his own.

TEACHING IDEA

- Ask students to write a postcard to a friend or relative from the first-person point of view.

INTERDISCIPLINARY CONNECTIONS

- Read and discuss other books by Mark Teague featuring Mrs. LaRue and Ike, including *Detective LaRue: Letters From the Investigation*, 2004, and *LaRue Across America: Postcards From the Vacation*, 2011, both published by Scholastic. Have students compare these to *Dear Mrs. LaRue: Letters From Obedience School.*
- Conduct a letter-writing campaign. Have students write friendly or persuasive letters to friends or to their local paper. Read other letter-writing mentor texts for models.

The Extraordinary Mark Twain (According to Susy)

Written by Barbara Kerley
Illustrated by Edwin Fotheringham
Scholastic Press, 2010, 72 pp.

In a masterful work Barbara Kerley weaves 13-year-old Susy Clemens's biography of her famous father, Samuel Clemens into a story about how to write a biography. Using excerpts from Susy's journals, complete with her misspellings and unique perceptions, Kerley unveils a portrait of Mark Twain that includes a glimpse into his public and private lives, his eccentricities, his humor, and his roles as a family man, father, and husband. Through Kerley's impeccable research, fascinating facts about Twain are revealed. Back matter includes author's notes on both Samuel and Susy Clemens, a guide for writing a biography, a time line of Twain's life, and a detailed list of sources. The various perspectives in this book make it perfect for teaching point of view.

TEACHING IDEA

- In order to guide students in determining how the point of view helps them to relate to the characters, invite them to analyze two sample passages from the book (e.g. one written in the first-person point of view and the other written in third-person point of view). Guide students to carefully look for the identifying pronouns used by the narrator and why one point of view is more effective than the other: Ask: *What point of view did they use in their writing? How do they know? Which character's point of view is used?* During writing workshop, ask students to apply this new information to their own drafts.

INTERDISCIPLINARY CONNECTION

- Bring in several different copies of news stories or magazines. Ask students to read various articles about the same story, but from different sources. In small groups, invite students to discuss the differences between the stories or if the stories are biased toward one particular point of view. As a follow-up activity, invite students to create a unit-of-study newspaper to explore writing from different points of view.

I Am the Dog, I Am the Cat

Written by Donald Hall
Illustrated by Barry Moser
Dial, 1994, 32 pp.

In alternating voices, the dog and the cat share their likes, dislikes, and other observations about one another and their owners. Readers will find the cat's and dog's points of view very humorous. The story is accompanied by watercolor portraits. Try partnering this book with *Joyful Noises: Poems for Two Voices* by Paul Fleischman.

TEACHING IDEA

- Invite students to write a two-voice story about two different animals, people, or objects.

INTERDISCIPLINARY CONNECTION

- Ask students to read and research factual information about cat and dog behaviors.

The Little Red Pen

Written by Janet Stevens and Susan Stevens Crummel
Illustrated by Janet Stevens
Harcourt, 2011, 56 pp.

Initially following the plot of *The Little Red Hen*, the authors introduce a high-spirited red pen with too many papers to grade. This pen encourages the other office supplies to give her assistance, but they only share excuse after excuse. The Little Red Pen decides to take charge and correct all of the papers herself until she is utterly exhausted and lands in the "Pit of No Return" (also known as the trash). The other office supplies finally realize that they need to save her so that all of the homework gets graded. With ample humor and wordplay, this story boasts many opportunities for creative writing.

TEACHING IDEA

- Before reading the book, invite students to preview it online at www.youtube.com/watch?v=xlVSwfglD6g. Then ask them to retell another familiar tale from the point of view of a character different from the one whose viewpoint is represented in the traditional version. Encourage students to capture the main characters' feelings and use a distinctive voice so that their readers will gain a new understanding of their story.

INTERDISCIPLINARY CONNECTION

- Encourage students to create a Readers Theater script and perform it for the class.

Mirror Mirror

Written by Marilyn Singer
Illustrated by Josée Masse
Dutton, 2010, 32 pp.

Author/poet Marilyn Singer has created her own form of poetry—the *reverso*. First, you read the poem down the page in the usual way. Then, when you read the same poem up the page—reverso—you have a new poem and a new point of view. Singer offers an explanation of how she created the form and even includes her first reverso, about her cat. This outstanding collection of reverso poems includes familiar tales, such as *Sleeping Beauty*, *Cinderella*, and *Rumpelstiltskin*, to consider the character's point of view. The detailed illustrations are cleverly divided down the middle to provide a visual insight to the various points of views in each fairy tale reverso.

TEACHING IDEAS

- Ask students to talk with a partner to describe the voice of several different viewpoints. Discuss how the voice changes as each poem is read in reverse and how the author utilizes punctuation and/or capitalization to vary the voice.
- Invite students to use the poet's creative form to compose their own reverso poetry based on familiar stories or daily events.

INTERDISCIPLINARY CONNECTION

- Ask students to create illustrations for their poems to display either in print or online form.

A Place Where Hurricanes Happen

Written by Renée Watson
Illustrated by Shadra Strickland
Random House, 2010, 40 pp.

In a close-knit New Orleans neighborhood, four friends and their families enjoy their day. Then Hurricane Katrina hits, and the children find themselves separated. In alternating voices, the four children describe their lives before, during, and after the storm. Each family copes with the storm in a very different way, and even through the devastation, they remain hopeful and resilient. The children all agree, "We're from New Orleans, a place where hurricanes happen. But that's only the bad side." The lyrical free verse is splendidly matched with Shadra Strickland's vivid mixed-media paintings.

TEACHING IDEA

- Use the Open-Mind Portrait strategy (Tompkins, 2001; McLaughlin & Allen, 2002) to create and represent personal meanings for the story. The strategy enables students to understand a character's perspective or point of view.

INTERDISCIPLINARY CONNECTIONS

- Ask students to use a hand-map graphic organizer to brainstorm events where they have experienced feelings of fear, nervousness, excitement, anger, or happiness. Have them focus on one of these experiences to describe their emotions in a personal narrative.
- Encourage students to learn more about natural disasters, using expository reading materials.

Romeow and Drooliet

Written and illustrated by Nina Laden
Chronicle Books, 2005, 44 pp.

In this parody of the Shakespeare classic *Romeo and Juliet*, a cat (Romeow) and a dog (Drooliet) fall in love and are secretly married by a mouse. This version has a much happier ending and can be used to explore the different characters' points of view.

TEACHING IDEA

- Form small writing-circle groups and invite students to compose a play with two different points of view.

INTERDISCIPLINARY CONNECTION

- Read other literature selections that highlight parody. After reading, ask students to create their own Readers Theater parody script to perform.

The Secret Knowledge of Grown-Ups

Written and illustrated by David Wisniewski
Lothrop, Lee & Shepard, 1998, 48 pp.

In this satirical picture book, the author decides to reveal the truth behind all the rules that parents seem to impose upon kids. The book cleverly resembles a secret file with pages of worn-out adult sayings, such as "Grown-up Rule #31: Eat your vegetables. The Official Reason is that they are good for you." When they turn the page, readers learn the truth. The unusual presentation will appeal to all readers. This is an excellent mentor text to use for point of view and to discuss the author's writing style.

TEACHING IDEA

- Ask students to write rules that they would share with their parents/guardians. Encourage them to provide reasons for these rules and then work with a partner to write a page for a rule book.

INTERDISCIPLINARY CONNECTION

- Invite students to write about everyday rules in an imaginative and unexpected way. After brainstorming the rules that they have heard from adults at home and at school, ask students to deliberate on the reasons for these rules. Then, ask them to create a Readers Theater script about a new community with rules and the reasons that these rules are needed for the town to operate smoothly.

Terezin: Voices From the Holocaust
Written by Ruth Thompson
Candlewick, 2011, 64 pp.

Terezin was a concentration camp that imprisoned thousands of Jewish children, many of whom were transferred from the overcrowded Auschwitz. Of the 15,000 children that entered this camp, fewer than 100 would survive. The author shares a personal look at these children using diaries, artwork, oral histories, and quotations from the survivors. Through documentation secretly recorded by artists and writers, and the diaries of children and adults, the reader experiences the true impact of the camp. The layout of the book is attractive, including sidebars that expand on the text, an index, a glossary, and an interesting time line. The material is well documented with source notes. A useful primary source website is listed: www.azrielifoundation.org/memoirs/.

TEACHING IDEA

■ Encourage students to pay close attention to the artwork and quotations throughout this nonfiction text. Ask them to write a letter from the point of view of one of the children.

INTERDISCIPLINARY CONNECTIONS

■ Partner this text with other books pertaining to the Holocaust.

■ Using an inquiry approach, ask students to frame questions and to find resources to guide their inquiries.

When I Met the Wolf Girls
Written by Deborah Noyes
Illustrated by August Hall
Houghton Mifflin, 2007, 40 pp.

In this picture book based on a true story, readers learn about two feral girls who were brought into an orphanage from the jungles of India. The story is presented from the perspective of a young girl named Bulu, who shares how the "wolf girls" are tamed and domesticated through love and kindness. Told through free verse, this story will spark further interest in learning about the history of these girls. The author includes a photograph of the girls and some historical notes and resources to support further inquiry.

TEACHING IDEA

■ With partners, ask students to assume the voice of the wolf girls and compose a letter to the Reverend, describing their life before arriving at the orphanage.

INTERDISCIPLINARY CONNECTIONS

■ Invite students to learn more about orphaned children and the adjustments they must make to fit into a new environment.

The Wolf's Story: What Really Happened to Little Red Riding Hood?
Written by Toby Forward
Illustrated by Izhar Cohen
Candlewick, 2005, 32 pp.

This clever retelling of *Little Red Riding Hood* is told from the wolf's perspective. Throughout this version, the wolf wants you to believe that he was framed, that it was never his fault (e.g., "I did nothing wrong." "Would I lie to you?" "It was the old woman who started it." "Like, I'm frightening?").

The wolf spends so much of the book trying to persuade the reader that by the end, you cannot trust him. Since the wolf distorts the truth, this book is certainly useful to teach perspective and irony in writing.

TEACHING IDEA

■ As a class, brainstorm a variety of familiar folk tales and ask students to select a character whose perspective they'd like to share. Students should write an original tale from that point of view.

INTERDISCIPLINARY CONNECTIONS

■ The book serves as an excellent mentor text for writing and drama. For example, ask students to create a Readers Theater script to perform for others, using the new version of their chosen tale. Students can also write a new ending to the story.

■ Encourage students to read nonfiction books about wolves to learn facts about their behavior and habitat.

POINT OF VIEW AND THE AMERICAN FLAG

When I pledge allegiance to the flag each day, I think about my dad, who is serving in Iraq. I am filled with pride as I think about Dad protecting the freedom of every person in all 50 states across our country. Sometimes, though, I am afraid because the red stripes remind me of the blood Dad's friends have lost from their war wounds. Silently I pray Dad will be safe.

In each classroom across the United States of America, students recite the Pledge of Allegiance to the American flag each morning. The 13 alternating red and white stripes on this flag represent the original colonies. Inside the blue rectangle in the flag's upper left-hand corner are 50 white stars that represent each state.

POINT OF VIEW REFERENCE CHART

Name: ______________________________

Study the definition provided for each type of point of view. With a partner, confirm that your understanding of the definition is clear. Use this information to help you identify the point of view used in *Back of the Bus* by Aaron Reynolds and in *Rosa's Bus: The Ride to Civil Rights* by Jo S. Kittinger.

POINT OF VIEW	DEFINITION	EXAMPLE
First Person	One of the characters tells the story, using the pronoun, *I*.	I ran the mile in gym class and was happy I finished in less than ten minutes. That is a great time for me, but boy do I stink! I hope no one will notice the stench when I get to class. Oh no. I have math. I sit next to Jada, the cutest cheerleader on the squad!
Third-Person Limited	A story is told through the eyes of a single character using third-person pronouns, such as *he* and *she*. The point of view is limited because the reader only sees the event from that character's point of view.	Justin ran the mile in gym class. He was happy to finish in less than ten minutes. He smelled foul and hoped that no one would notice the stench when he got to class. When he arrived in math class and sat down, he thought he saw Jada move her seat away from him.
Third-Person Omniscient	Someone outside the story is observing the characters and events and reporting what can be seen and heard. This all-knowing narrator can see into the hearts and minds of all the characters and show what they think and feel.	Justin was thinking about how happy he was when he ran the mile in under ten minutes. Although he was worried that he smelled, he headed to math class, where he saw Jada, the cutest cheerleader on the squad. Jada had no idea that Justin liked her and thought she was cute. All she knew was that he smelled and she had to get away.
Third-Person Objective	A story or event is related by someone who is not involved and who reports only what can be seen and heard. It does *not* show what the characters think and feel. Often this point of view is used in newspaper articles, textbooks, and nonfiction works.	Justin ran the mile in less than ten minutes. He headed to math class and sat next to Jada, a cheerleader. She moved her desk away from him.

WHAT'S THE POINT OF VIEW?

Name: ______________________________

Read the excerpts below from *Back of the Bus* and *Rosa's Bus: The Ride to Civil Rights*. Using the clues in the text, identify the point of view and explain how you arrived at your answer. Refer to the Point of View Reference Chart to help you.

TITLE OF THE STORY	THE TEXT	POINT OF VIEW	HOW I KNOW
Back of the Bus by Aaron Reynolds	"Winter's here in Montgomery, but I got the window down . . ." (page 4) "Mama shakes a 'no' at me, and I hold [the marble] snug in my hand." (page 9)		
Rosa's Bus: The Ride to Civil Rights by Jo S. Kittinger	"The bus left the General Motors factory in Michigan and headed for Terre Haute, Indiana, where it carried folks for several years before moving south to Alabama in 1954." (page 6) "[Black people] walked for 382 days. That's how long they boycotted the buses." (page 29)		

TWO VIEWPOINTS

Name: ______________________________

Listen to your teacher read different descriptions of how Rosa Parks refused to move to the back of the bus. Record what you have learned about the event from each narrator's perspective in the appropriate spaces below. Afterward, answer the question at the bottom of the page.

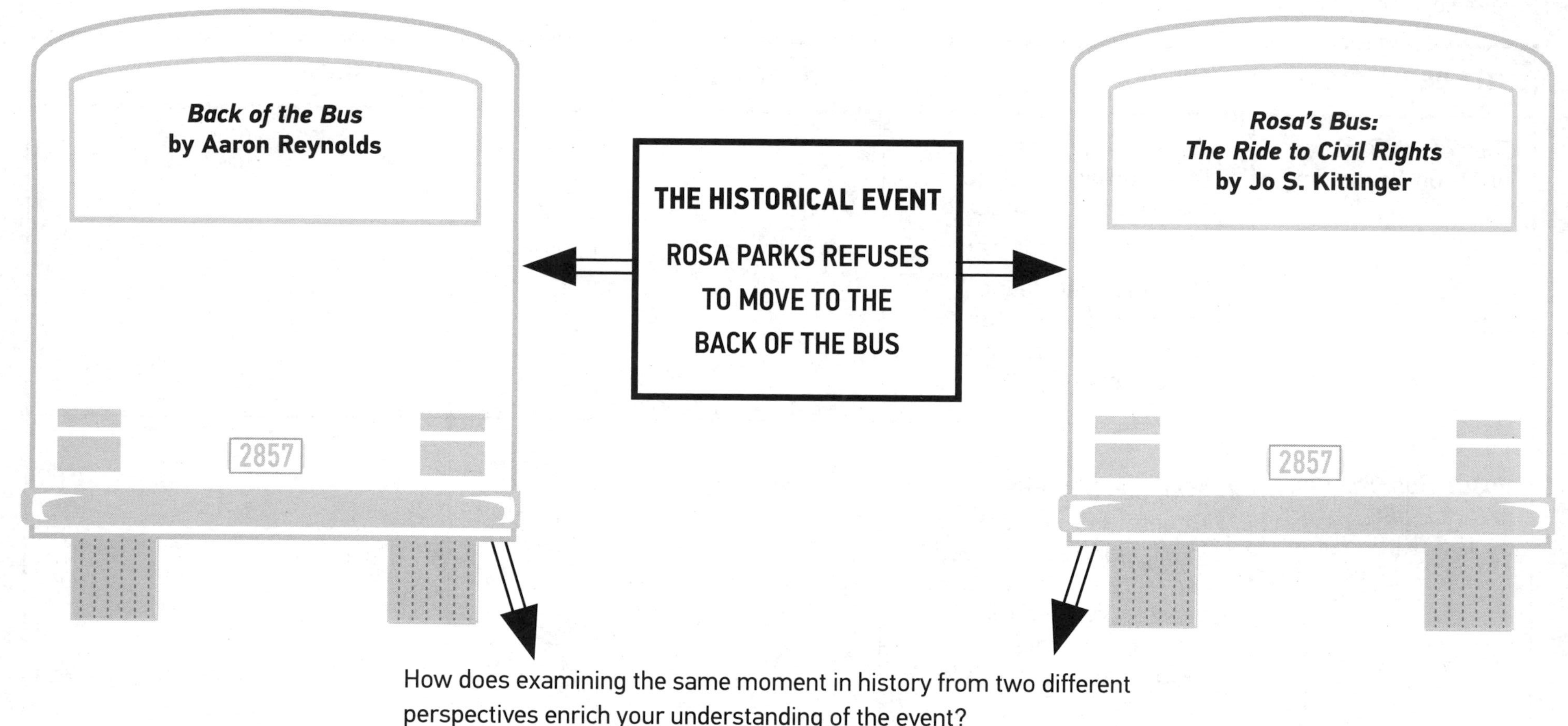

How does examining the same moment in history from two different perspectives enrich your understanding of the event?

____

____

____

____

POINT OF VIEW IMPROV

You are the egg. The person holding you approaches a hot pan bubbling with oil. What do you say?

You are the cat and your family member is scratching your ears. Express your feelings in words.

You are a nose. You have a cold and are stuffed up. What would you like to say to your owner?

You are a thorn on a rosebush. Someone is trying to pick your rose. What do you say to him?

You are a cheeseburger. You see a big mouth coming towards you. What do you call out?

You are a cell phone with buttons worn down from constant texting. Your owner pulls you from his pocket for the 100th time that day. What do you say to make him stop?

You are a Chihuahua who has just fallen in love with an elephant. What do you say to get the elephant's attention and convince him that your love is meant to be?

You are a book and you want everyone in your class to read you. How can you advertise yourself?

You are a warm glove, and you see a person's freezing cold hand. What would you say to get her to put you on her hand? How will you let her know you can help her?

You are a stomach who has not eaten since breakfast, and you smell a very delicious aroma coming from a pizza shop as your owner walks by. What do you say to get him to stop?

MODEL SCRIPT FOR DIFFERENT POINTS OF VIEW

Name: ______________________________

POINT OF VIEW FOR SCENE	CHARACTERS FOR SCENE	THE SCENE
Emphasize the toothbrush's point of view or perspective	Stewart's toothbrush—Mr. T. Stewart's dental floss—Flossie Stewart Sweet Tooth	Toothbrush torture (page 22)

TOOTHBRUSH TORTURE

MR. T.: Oh noooo! Please, Stewart, have a heart! Don't let that bully of a tooth attack me again!

STEWART: Calm down, Mr. T. We're winning this battle. That ol' sweet tooth will be outta here before ya know it!

SWEET TOOTH: HEY, KID, ENOUGH ALREADY! You sic Mr. T. on me again, and this here molar will tear out his bristles one by one!

FLOSSIE: Oh yeah, mister tough guy? Try it, and I'll irritate your gum so badly you won't sleep for a week!

STEWART: Calm down, you guys. You're wreckin' my concentration. The big game is tomorrow, and I gotta zero in on my moves.

SWEET TOOTH: Well, buster, if ya want any peace and quiet, GET THOSE TEETH WHACKERS OUTTA HERE NOW!

MR. T.: You think I like removin' your scummy plaque? In all my born days, I've never seen a tooth as dirty as you. To top it off, ya smell like the inside of a dumpster.

FLOSSIE: Yeah, ya big, rotten cavity.

SWEET TOOTH: Are you gonna let these guys keep abusin' me, Stewart? Come on, kid. Listen to me, or you'll be sorry!

STEWART: They're just givin' ya a taste of your own medicine. Nothin' I can do about it.

SWEET TOOTH: Yowsers! Stop it with the bristles already!

MR. T.: Come on, Flossie! Lasso him and yank hard! He is almost outta here!

FLOSSIE: Prepare to rest in peace, Sweet Tooth.

SCENES FROM *SWEET TOOTH*: DIFFERENT POINTS OF VIEW

POINT OF VIEW FOR SCENE 1	CHARACTERS FOR SCENE 1	SCENE 1
Emphasize the bride's perspective or point of view	The bride The crying child The bride's grandfather Sweet Tooth	The wedding cake fiasco (pages 5–6)

POINT OF VIEW FOR SCENE 2	CHARACTERS FOR SCENE 2	SCENE 2
Emphasize the principal's perspective or point of view	The principal A student in the class Stewart Sweet Tooth	Too many detentions (page 7)

POINT OF VIEW FOR SCENE 3	CHARACTERS FOR SCENE 3	SCENE 3
Emphasize the perspective or point of view of the boy holding the gummy bears	Boy with the gummy bears Girl saying, "SHHHHHHHH!!!!!" Stewart Sweet Tooth	Movie interruptions (pages 9–10)

POINT OF VIEW FOR SCENE 4	CHARACTERS FOR SCENE 4	SCENE 4
Emphasize the perspective or point of view of the half-eaten chocolate bunny	The half-eaten chocolate bunny Allison (Stewart's sister) Stewart Sweet Tooth	The Easter basket disaster (page 11)

POINT OF VIEW FOR SCENE 5	CHARACTERS FOR SCENE 5	SCENE 5
Emphasize Stewart's teammate's point of view or perspective	Stewart's teammate The umpire Stewart Sweet Tooth	The infamous strike out (page 24)

CHAPTER 3 • PLOT

"But no matter how much we begged, my dad would never come into the water."

—from *Testing the Ice* (page 7)

A plot is the underlying sequence of events to explain the "why" for the things that happen in the story. The plot draws the reader into the characters' lives and allows the reader to understand the choices that the characters make.

A plot's structure is the way in which the story elements are arranged. Writers compose their stories and vary the structure depending on the needs of the story. There are various elements that align with plot development:

- Exposition refers to the information needed to understand the story.
- Complication is the catalyst that originates the major conflict.
- Climax refers to the turning point in the story. This occurs when characters aim to resolve the conflict.
- Resolution is the series of events that resolve or bring the story to a full close.

In order to understand and explore the basic plot structure, students need multiple opportunities to interact with text. It's also helpful for them to use a plot diagram to plug in the various elements they encounter as they read.

LESSON 5

Plot Structure

MODEL TEXT

The Best Beekeeper of Lalibela: A Tale From Africa
Written by Cristina Kessler
Illustrated by Leonard Jenkins
Holiday House, 2006, 32 pp.

This Notable Books for Global Society award recipient is a timeless tale of a young girl's determination to follow her dream. Young Almaz, who lives in a mountain village in Ethiopia, loves the honey that she purchases at the market. Yet, she is determined to become the best beekeeper in the village, even though it is considered "men's work." Her courage to overcome gender barriers enables her to devise a creative way to maintain her hives. With the encouragement of the local priest, she learns the art of beekeeping and is soon outselling others at the market. The author skillfully infuses information about Ethiopian culture and tradition and includes a glossary in the back.

MATERIALS

- 1 copy of *The Best Beekeeper of Lalibela*
- copies of No Homework (page 42; 1 copy per student)
- copies of Exploring Plot (page 43; 1 copy per student and a transparency or scanned copy to project onto a screen)
- copies of PLOT Acrostic (page 44; 1 copy per student)

CRITICAL QUESTION

How does a reader analyze plot structure?

WARM-UP

Form groups of three or four students. Distribute a copy of No Homework to each group. Read the scenario aloud. Next, direct students to identify the narrator's problem and her goal. Then, ask students to list three obstacles that prevent the narrator from achieving her goal. Finally, instruct students to generate ideas for overcoming each obstacle they listed in order to help the narrator attain her goal.

As a class, discuss students' responses. Compare and contrast their ideas for attaining the goal of making honor roll. Which ones will work best? Why? Which ones might fail? Why?

STEP BY STEP

1. Explain that, like the narrator in No Homework, Almaz, the protagonist in the tale *The Best Beekeeper of Lalibela*, has a problem and a goal. As she strives to attain her goal, she also encounters obstacles but eventually overcomes them and learns from them.
2. Before reading the story aloud, ask students to pay attention to Almaz's problem, her goal, the obstacles she faces, and the way she overcomes these obstacles. Instruct students to jot down some of the obstacles Almaz faces as they listen to the story.
3. Using a document camera, project a copy of the text onto the screen, or hold open the book for all to see. Read aloud the story.
4. After reading the story, distribute the reproducible Exploring Plot. Direct students to think about the tale and identify the following components of the story:
   - Almaz's goal
   - the big problem
   - events that are obstacles to her goal
   - events that help her attain her goal
   - the resolution to Almaz's problem
   - what she learns from overcoming the obstacles and achieving her goal
5. Provide time for students to complete the Exploring Plot graphic organizer. Students should write their thoughts in the hives and the honeycomb. Here are some potential responses:

   GOAL:
   To produce the best honey in Lalibela
   PROBLEM:
   Almaz does not know how to be a beekeeper.
   EVENTS THAT HINDER:
   - Men in village say beekeeping is men's work, not women's.
   - Almaz cannot climb the trees to reach the hive.
   - Ants turn Almaz's hive into a mud mound.

   EVENTS THAT HELP:
   - The priest declares that Almaz can keep bees.
   - Almaz discovers a way to make honey.
   - Almaz sees her brother pulling a tomato paste can filled with water.

   RESOLUTION/OUTCOME:
   Almaz puts 4 table legs in tomato paste cans filled with water. The ants drown; the bees thrive; and Almaz makes the best honey in Lalibela.
   WHAT ALMAZ LEARNS:
   Almaz learns that accomplishing a goal requires great effort. She also learns that to find solutions to problems, one needs to observe his/her surroundings.
6. Project a transparency or scanned copy of Exploring Plot onto a screen. Ask students to share their responses and record them. Instruct students to revise, change, and add ideas when needed.

WRAP-UP

Distribute the PLOT Acrostic to students. Review the directions and provide time for students to write.

To share their acrostics, ask students to pass their poems to someone near them. Then tell students to read the poem and pass it to someone else nearby. Keep "poem swapping" until students have read three or four poems. Here is a sample acrostic:

Problems face the protagonist.
Lots of events complicate the problem.
Obstacles arise.
Thoughtful solutions lead to achieving a goal.

LESSON 6

Investigating Conflict

MODEL TEXT

The Memory Coat
Written by Elvira Woodruff
Illustrated by Michael Dooling
Scholastic, 1999, 32 pp.

This historical fiction book is a moving story about a multigenerational Jewish family immigrating to the United States from Russia during the reign of Tsar Nicholas I. The emotional hardships endured by this family are depicted through the author's words and the oil illustrations. The most challenging part of their journey is the inspection station at Ellis Island. The family encourages cousin Grisha to wear a new coat instead of the tattered one that he refuses to take off. The inspector put an "E" on his coat (meaning "eye trouble," usually associated with the dreaded disease of trachoma) because he did not understand their language and conversation and didn't bother to find an interpreter to translate the situation. Rachel's quick thinking—and the coat—keep the family together and the story leaves readers wondering how they will adjust in their new surroundings.

CRITICAL QUESTION

How does a reader investigate conflict and examine its effect on characters?

WARM-UP

Inform students that they are going to describe a conflict they have experienced. Remind them that the conflict can be a simple one, such as an argument with a parent or a problem with a friend. In addition to describing the problem, ask students to explain how it was resolved or if it was resolved. Ask them to think about what they learned from the conflict.

Distribute copies of the Conflict Connection page. Provide time for students to write. Ask them to share this journal entry with a partner.

MATERIALS

- 1 copy of *The Memory Coat*
- copies of Conflict Connection (page 45; 1 copy per student)
- chart paper
- copies of Investigate a Conflict (page 46; 1 copy per student)
- copies of Wrap Up in Whispered Stories (page 47; 1 copy per student)

STEP BY STEP

1. Explain to students that story characters grow and learn from the conflicts they experience, just as we do. Inform students that in today's lesson they will focus on exploring conflict.
2. Define conflict as a class. (*Conflict is the problem that starts the action moving forward.*)
3. Discuss and provide examples of types of conflict found in literature: person vs. person; person vs. nature; person vs. society; person vs. self. Remind students that conflicts can take place inside a character's head, such as when he or she experiences fear, doubt, or indecision.
4. Using a document camera, project a copy of *The Memory Coat* onto a screen or simply open the book for all to see as you read aloud. Ask students to listen for the different conflicts that occur in the story and be ready to discuss them.
5. After reading *The Memory Coat*, brainstorm a list of the conflicts in the story and record them on chart paper. Ask students to choose one of the conflicts on the list to explore how the conflict affects the character. Before students make their choices, remind them to select a conflict that is meaty enough to analyze.
6. Distribute Investigate Conflict to students.
7. First, direct students to describe the conflict and explain why it happens.

DESCRIBE THE CONFLICT *(Who or what is involved?)*	**REASON CONFLICT OCCURS**	**RESOLUTION/OUTCOME** *(Does the problem continue, or is it resolved?)*	**EFFECT CONFLICT HAS ON CHARACTER(S)**
Grisha is overcome with grief and mourns his parents' deaths.	Grisha becomes an orphan when his parents die in an epidemic.	Grisha isolates himself and runs behind the synagogue to grieve. Rachel and the memories of his mother's love comfort him.	Grisha changes when his parents die. He becomes lonely and depressed.

8. Next, instruct students to explore the outcome of or resolution to the conflict. Remind students that the resolution to a conflict is not always a solution to a problem. For example, Grisha refuses to let Rachel's mother and their grandmother make him a new coat. His resolution to the problem (*not accepting their offer*) does not solve his problem of freezing in the winter.
9. Finally, guide students to consider how the conflict develops or changes the character. Ask: *How does he/she grow? What does he/she learn?* If students need more guidance in exploring a conflict, model the example in the chart above.
10. Provide time for students to complete the Investigate Conflict activity.
11. To share their explorations, ask students to find someone who investigated a different conflict. You can repeat this, if desired, so students can share with two or three others.

WRAP-UP

Explain to students that our country is made up of immigrants from every country in the world, and that family stories are for cherishing and saving. Invite them to try to find out about their family's history and their relatives' arrival in this country. Ask them if there are any "whispered stories that can be heard no more" (page 27) in their homes. As students talk to family members, instruct them to identify the conflicts the family faced as they immigrated to America.

Send home the Wrap Up in Whispered Stories activity page. Ask students to gather their stories and bring them back to school to share with the class.

More Books for Teaching PLOT

Aunt Chip and the Great Triple Creek Dam Affair

Written and illustrated by Patricia Polacco
Philomel Books, 1996, 40 pp.

A perfect read-aloud during "Turn off your television week," this story explains a town that is so hooked on watching television that they have forgotten the pleasure of reading books and enjoying life. Aunt Chip remains unaffected by television and remains true to her old ways of sharing stories and teaching folks how to enjoy reading books.

TEACHING IDEA

- Draw a "plot mountain" to show the different components of plot (problem, climax, solution, and so on). Ask students to work together to complete the chart in order to review the definitions and to identify the conflict.

INTERDISCIPLINARY CONNECTION

- Ask students to write a slogan that encourages friends and family to read more books instead of watching television.

Brothers
Written by Yin
Illustrated by Chris Soentpiet
Philomel, 2006, 32 pp.

In this beautifully illustrated picture book, a Chinese immigrant, Young Ming, arrives in San Francisco during the days of the construction of the transcontinental railroad. Ming learns that one of his brothers has gone to work on the railroad, leaving him no choice but to work with another brother, Shek, in his grocery store in Chinatown. The economic times are tough, so Shek leaves Ming in charge of the store to find another job. Ming is warned not to leave Chinatown alone, so he wears a disguise and makes friends with Patrick. The two boys learn that they have many things in common and soon business starts to improve. The two friends have such a strong friendship that they view themselves as "brothers." The book contains an afterword with further information about Irish and Chinese immigration to San Francisco in the mid-1800s.

TEACHING IDEA
- Ask students to think about what might have taken place before this story began and to write a prologue. Tell them to focus on the major problem of the characters. Have students talk with a partner about what caused the problem and how the problem was resolved.

INTERDISCIPLINARY CONNECTIONS
- Encourage students to use the information from the afterword to conduct an inquiry about immigration in the 1800s.
- Have students read Yin's sequel, *Coolies*, to learn what happened to Ming's brothers.

Crossing Bok Chitto: A Choctaw Tale of Friendship & Freedom
Written by Tim Tingle
Illustrated by Jeanne Rorex Bridges
Cinco Puntos Press, 2006, 40 pp.

In the 1800s, there was a river in Mississippi known as Bok Chitto. On one side of the river lived the Choctaws, a nation of Indian people, and on the opposite side lived the plantation owners and their slaves. According to the laws of the time, if a slave crossed over the river, he or she would be free. In this story, a young girl named Martha crosses the river and meets a young slave boy named Little Mo. When Martha learns that Little Mo's family is in trouble, she helps them cross Bok Chitto to freedom.

TEACHING IDEA
- Prepare sentence strips or paper slips with the main components of the story. Have students work together in small groups to visually represent the traditional rising-action plot.

INTERDISCIPLINARY CONNECTIONS
- Students can compose a paragraph to explain why Martha Tom helped Little Mo and his family cross the river.
- This selection is ideal to include in a text set about Native American culture, especially when focusing on strong bonds and friendship.

The Great Race
Written by David Bouchard
Illustrated by Zhong-Yang Huang
Roundhouse, 1997, 32 pp.

This beautifully illustrated fable about the origins of the Chinese zodiac will leave readers pondering questions and answers after multiple readings. A grandmother teaches her youngest granddaughter the importance of the order of the animals in the zodiac and how this order came to be determined through a great race. The book also contains information about the zodiac and each of the twelve animals' characteristics and symbols.

TEACHING IDEA

■ Ask small groups of students to make comic strips of the main events in the story. Use the illustrations to document the rise of action and excitement on a plot line graph.

INTERDISCIPLINARY CONNECTION

■ Students can learn more about the animals that make up the Chinese Zodiac while learning about related customs and traditions of the culture.

Henry and the Kite Dragon

Written by Bruce Edward Hall
Illustrated by William Low
Philomel Books, 2004, 32 pp.

In this historical-fiction picture book, readers will meet eight-year old Henry Chu. Henry's favorite thing to do is to help his Grandfather Chin create beautiful and intricate kites and to fly them. The story takes place in New York City's Chinatown in the 1920s, where Henry has to tolerate kids from the other neighborhood who throw rocks at one of Grandfather Chin's most precious kites. Eventually, though, the boys from the two neighborhoods come to a compromise and discover a mutual respect and appreciation for the kites and their cultures.

TEACHING IDEA

■ Use a pattern of a kite and ask students to decorate the front of the kite with symbols and images that represent the theme of the story. On the back of the kite, ask them to write about the conflict in the story and how the characters reached a resolution. Tell students to include the events that led to the resolution and to identify the type of conflict that appeared in the story.

INTERDISCIPLINARY CONNECTIONS

■ This is an excellent book for launching conversations about compromise and acceptance. It is also a perfect addition to a text set about bullying or one featuring Notable Books for a Global Society recipients.

■ This book serves as an effective launch to inquiries about kite-making and its history.

The Hungry Coat: A Tale From Turkey

Written and illustrated by Demi
Margaret K. McElderry Books, 2004, 40 pp.

In this award-winning folktale, a Turkish folk hero named Nasrettin Hoca, attends a friend's banquet in a tattered coat. He is immediately turned away from the event, which forces him to return home and change into his finest garments. When he returns to the banquet, he stuffs food and wine into his coat. When questioned why he feeds his garment, Nasrettin explains, "This shows it was the coat and not me that you invited to your banquet." The tale has a familiar moral that is rooted in traditional Turkish folklore. Demi's illustrations are inspired by Turkish art with geometric patterns.

TEACHING IDEA

■ Discuss the reaction of Nasrettin's friends at the banquet. Have students act out the scene in which Nasrettin walks into the banquet in his tattered coat while the other guests whisper and judge his appearance. Ask students to develop reasons for both sides of the argument regarding the conflict that Nasrettin should not have entered a banquet in a tattered coat. The other argument sheds light on the moral of the story that it should not matter what Nasrettin wore to the event, especially since he is a good friend. Afterward, ask students to plot the feelings of Nasrettin, his highs and lows, by means of a graph.

INTERDISCIPLINARY CONNECTION

■ Invite students to create their own folktale based on a story from their own lives. After creating individual stories with their own morals/lessons, encourage students to work with others to dramatize the tales for an audience.

My Mountain Song

Written by Shutta Crum
Illustrated by Ted Rand
Clarion, 2004, 32 pp.

On a summer day, Brenda hears her Gran Pap's mountain song and discovers that everyone born in the mountains has their own song. Brenda tries to reflect upon what memories she would include in her own mountain song, but gets interrupted by her pesky cousin and the neighbors. By accident, she hits Big Ma's favorite hen with dirt and stones. Brenda's guilt overshadows her song-writing progress, but eventually she composes her own mountain song.

TEACHING IDEAS

- Ask students to draw a storyboard to summarize the plot of the story.
- Have students talk with a partner about the significance of Brenda's frustration and her accidentally hurting her grandmother's hen.

INTERDISCIPLINARY CONNECTIONS

- Not only is this book suitable for exploring plot, but it also contains many examples of figurative language.
- This story takes place in the Appalachian Mountains, which may prompt further inquiry about the region.
- Ask students to compose their own song about their life, interests, or family.

Nothing Ever Happens on 90th Street

Written by Roni Schotter
Illustrated by Kyrsten Brooker
Orchard Books, 1997, 32 pp.

This Notable Children's Books in the Language Arts title is about a would-be writer named Eva. She faces the blank page and begins to write about everything that is happening around her, which she feels is "nothing." Everyone in her neighborhood stops to offer her writing advice, such as "Try to find poetry in your pudding," or "Stretch your imagination." When Eva takes matters into her own hands, she transforms the pages of her notebook into observations and stories that capture the energy of her neighborhood.

TEACHING IDEA

- After reading the story, ask students to identify the basic conflicts that are evident in the plot (person vs. self, person vs. environment, person vs. person, and so on). With a partner, students should describe the details and events that build toward the climax of the plot. Ask students to discuss how the author sets up tension and then resolves it.

INTERDISCIPLINARY CONNECTION

- Ask students to jot down some metaphors that the author uses to compare writing to something else. Then invite students to be observers of everyday activity in their neighborhood or playground in order to compose a new story entitled, "Nothing ever happens on . . . ."

The Secret River

Written by Marjorie Kinnan Rawlings
Illustrated by Leo and Diane Dillon
Atheneum Books for Young Readers, 2011, 56 pp.

Times are very desperate in Calpurnia's village, and there are no fish left in the rivers and streams. She is determined to find fish for her father to sell in his shop. Following the advice of her sage mother, Calpurnia follows her nose to a secret river full of beautiful and healthy fish. After seeking permission to catch and remove the fish from the river, she proudly hands them to her father. In her quest to help other members of the village, she also uses her resources for the betterment of everyone. The illustrations are elegant and capture the spirit and soul that embody the tale.

TEACHING IDEA

- Ask students to chart Calpurnia's change in response to each conflict. Create a four-column chart with the different types of plot conflict, including person vs. nature, person vs. person, person vs. self, and person vs. society. Ask students to work with a partner to write examples from the story that match each conflict and to note how the character changed.

INTERDISCIPLINARY CONNECTION

■ This book can also be used to teach the literary element of setting/atmosphere and contains unique language devices to reinforce word choice/voice. This particular book received a Newbery Honor medal in 1956 and has been reissued with stunning illustrations by Leo and Diane Dillon. It presents an excellent opportunity to conduct an illustrator study of the Dillons and to read and examine the artistic and literary craft in each of the works.

Spuds

Written by Karen Hesse
Illustrated by Wendy Watson
Scholastic, 2008, 32 pp.

In this historical-fiction picture book, three children work together to gather potatoes from a neighbor's field. They wait until their mother leaves for work, and gather three large sacks of what they thought were potatoes. They soon learn that the sacks were mostly full of stones and a few potatoes. Discouraged by the lack of food and the amount of trouble they were in when their mother found out, they had to return to the farm to apologize to Mr. Kennedy, the farmer. He was so happy to know that the stones had been removed that he allowed the children to keep the potatoes. In the end, the mother fries up the potatoes, and the children see that their home is one of love.

TEACHING IDEA

■ During reading, ask students to cite examples of how the author builds suspense. Ask them what writing techniques the author uses and then invite them to create a time line of events for the story, highlighting the climax.

INTERDISCIPLINARY CONNECTION

■ Invite students to discuss the theme of the book and for discussing issues of contemporary poverty and how they can help their community and neighbors.

Testing the Ice

Written by Sharon Robinson
Illustrated by Kadir Nelson
Scholastic Press, 2009, 40 pp.

In this inspirational story, testing the ice serves as a metaphor for Jackie Robinson's courage when he breaks the color barrier in professional baseball. Through this metaphor and story-within-a-story plot structure, Sharon Robinson unveils a highly personal portrait of her father that depicts his heroic qualities both on and off the ball field. Kadir Nelson's paintings mirror the greatness of the man, revealing him as both a competent, agile athlete; powerful leader; and a devoted father determined to protect his children even if it meant risking his own life.

TEACHING IDEA

■ Another way to explore plot is to incorporate drama. Invite student groups to present a scene from the book to the class and discuss how the author builds suspense.

INTERDISCIPLINARY CONNECTION

■ Jackie Robinson was a national sports hero and a personal hero to his family. Invite students to collect information about a hero of their own. Their hero can be an athlete, historical character, or family member. Provide materials for them to create poster-sized "baseball cards" of their hero, and display in the hallway or classroom.

NO HOMEWORK

Name: ______________________________

Identify the narrator's problem and ultimate goal. Then decide what obstacles prevent the narrator from attaining the goal. Finally, generate ideas to help the narrator attain the goal. Record your responses on the organizer below.

NO HOMEWORK SCENARIO

I can't believe I forgot my homework again! How will I ever make honor roll now? Even I don't know how I managed to miss four assignments in a row! I'm so forgetful, and my busy schedule doesn't help either. I must have searched through every stack of paper in my locker this morning trying to make sure that I didn't have any assignments that were due today. Man, I sure hope my grades are at least good enough to stay on the soccer team!

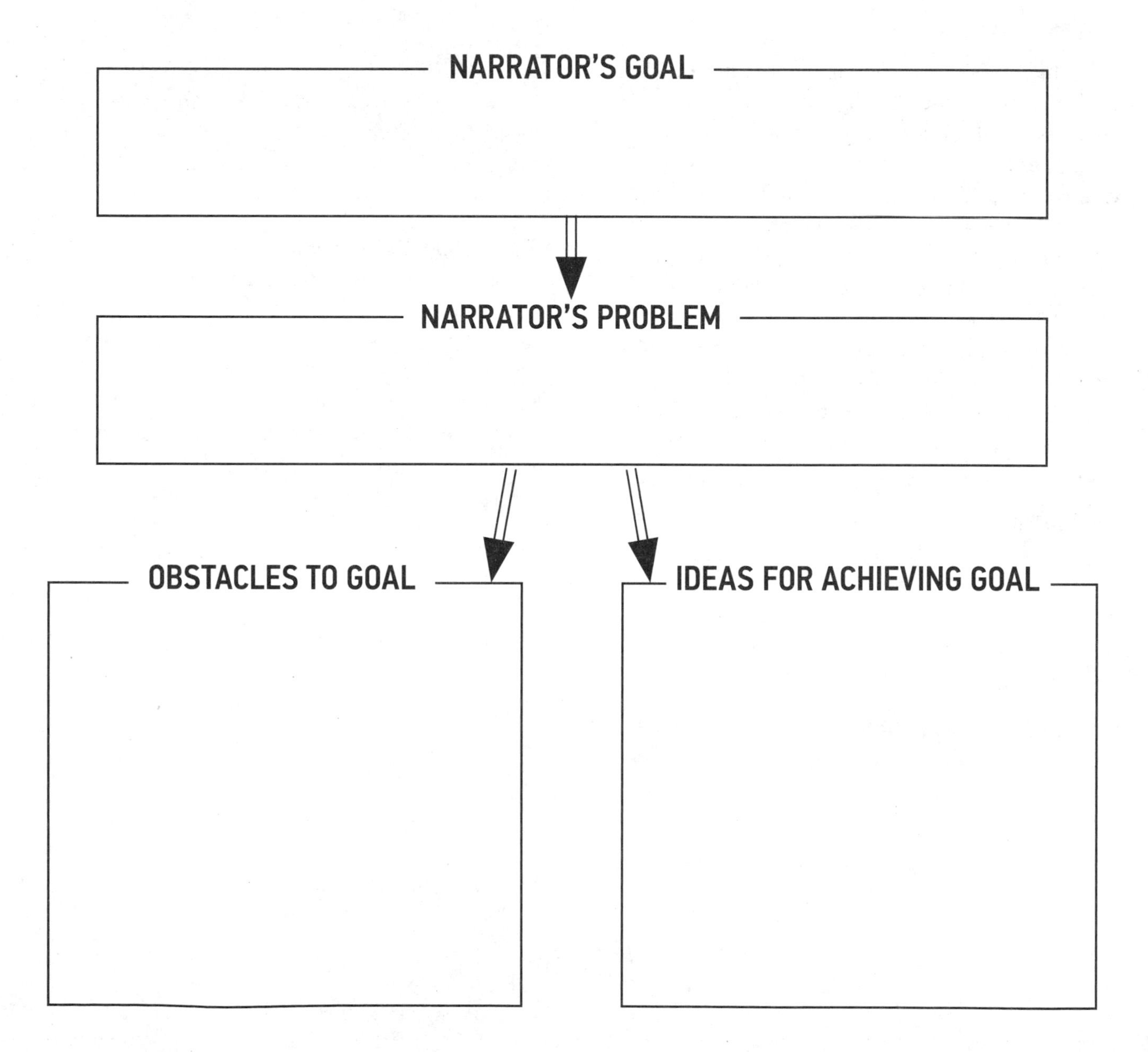

EXPLORING PLOT

Name: ____________________

Identify Almaz's goal and the problem she faces in attaining her goal. Next, list the events that are obstacles to her goal and the events that help her achieve her goal. Then state how the story ends, or what the outcome is. Finally, consider what Almaz learns from her experiences.

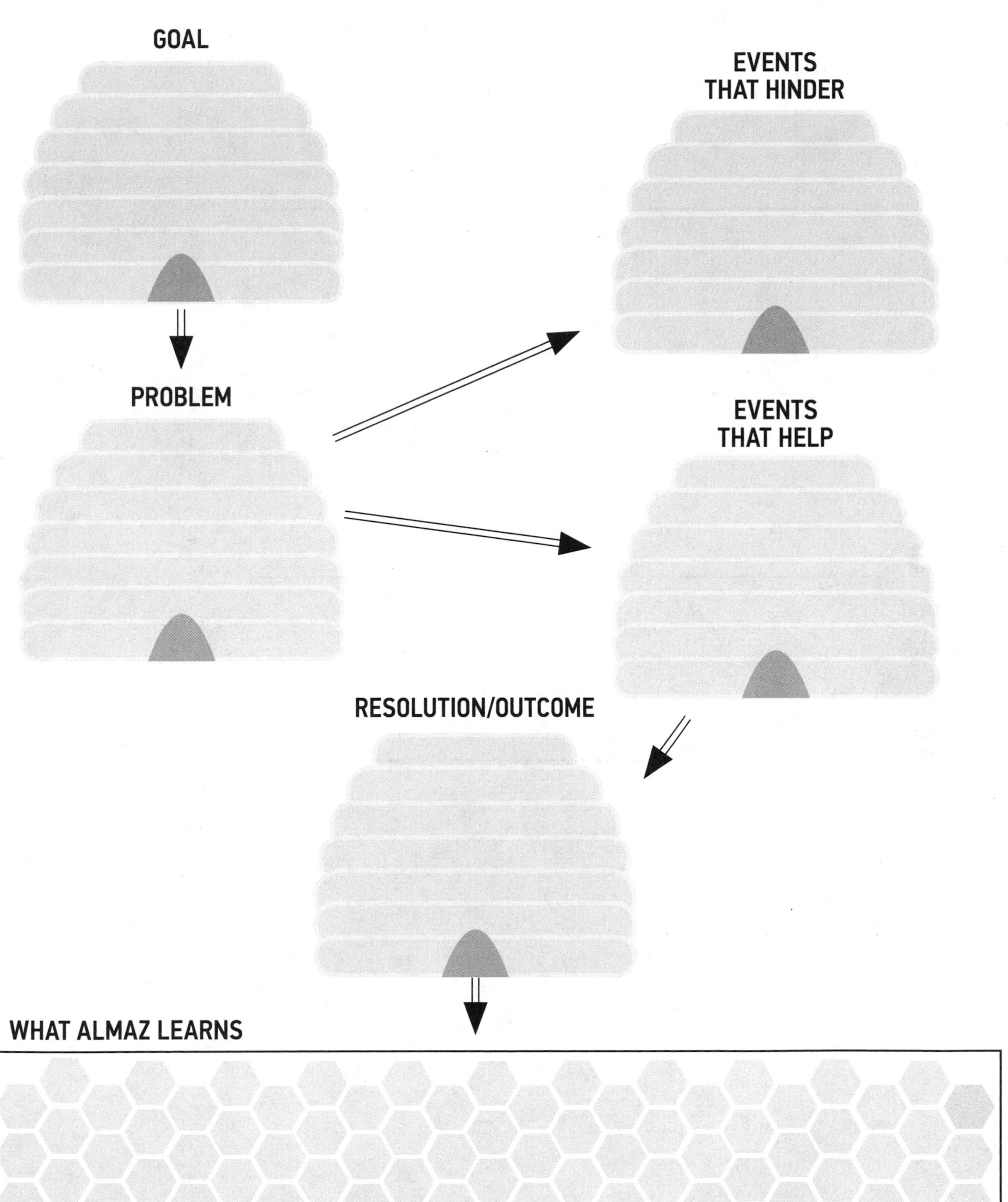

PLOT ACROSTIC

Name: ____

Create an acrostic poem that summarizes what you have learned about plot structure. Each letter below starts one line of the poem. After you finish writing your acrostic, illustrate it with pictures of key events from *The Best Beekeeper of Lalibela*.

P ____

L ____

O ____

T ____

CONFLICT CONNECTION

Name: ______________________

On the journal pages, write a paragraph about a conflict you have experienced. Do the following:

- Describe a conflict you have experienced.
- Discuss the outcome of the problem. Was the problem resolved or did it continue?
- Explain how the conflict affected you.
- Summarize what you learned from the conflict.

INVESTIGATE A CONFLICT

Name: ______________________________

Choose a conflict from *The Memory Coat* by Elvira Woodruff.

- Describe the conflict. Tell who or what is involved.
- Explain why the conflict happens.
- State the outcome of or resolution to the conflict.
- Consider how the characters grow and change because of the conflict. What do they learn?
- Write your responses in the chart below.

DESCRIBE THE CONFLICT	REASON CONFLICT OCCURS	RESOLUTION/OUTCOME	EFFECT CONFLICT HAS ON CHARACTER(S)

WRAP UP IN WHISPERED STORIES

Name: ______________________________

As you think about your family's story, consider the conflicts they might have had to face in the process of coming to America. On the coat patches, write down what you know about your family's experiences as they immigrated to America.

CHAPTER 4 • CHARACTERIZATION

"I cunningly observed them from the office window and was surprised to see them simply cross the road to the grand hotel. The sheer nerve of it. Holding their secret F. P. Club meeting right on the paper's doorstep. They probably think that's the last place anyone would look. I've got to get inside that building and find out what they're up to."

—From *Scoop! An Exclusive* (page 8)

Characterization is the method an author employs to create a character. Essentially the author uses six techniques to develop a character, including how the character interacts with others and what the character says, does, thinks, feels, and looks like.

Careful analysis of characters often involves making inferences based on the text. Moreover, observing characters' actions, what they learn, and how they change can also help readers discover the theme of the story. Thus, through character study, the reader deepens his or her comprehension of text.

LESSON 7

Analyzing Characters to Understand Author's Purpose

MODEL TEXT

The Spider and the Fly
Poem by Mary Howitt
Illustrated by Tony DiTerlizzi
Simon & Schuster, 2002, 40 pp.

This illustrated version of Mary Howitt's well-known poem explores the antics of a clever spider that preys on the vanity of an unsuspecting fly. DiTerlizzi manages to capture the idiosyncrasies of these two characters using black-and-white gouache in silver-and-black duotone. The cunning spider is shown with physical attributes such as a moustache and a handsome suit. On the other hand, the innocent fly is shown wearing a fringed flapper dress and batting her eyelashes. The marvelous details build suspense as the spider invites Miss Fly to "walk into his parlor," and unfortunately she falls victim to his cunning ways.

MATERIALS

- 1 copy of *The Spider and the Fly*
- copies of Cautionary Tales (page 57; 1 copy per student)
- markers and colored pencils
- copies of Character Web (page 58; 1 copy per student pair)
- timer

CRITICAL QUESTION

How does analyzing characterization inform the reader about the author's purpose?

WARM-UP

While holding up the book for the class to see, explain that although this picture book is recent, the words in this book are more than a hundred years old. The poet Mary Howitt wrote this "cautionary tale" in 1888.

Ask students to turn to a partner and quickly come up with a meaning for the term "cautionary tale." Invite students to share ideas with the class, directing the discussion toward an understanding that the author's purpose is to warn us about something. The author uses characters in the story to give us the warning, but it is up to us to find the warning message within their words and actions.

Distribute the reproducible Cautionary Tales. Read aloud the directions. Invite students to work in small groups to come up with several scenarios for cautionary tales. Here is a possible response for the first box:

> **EXAMPLE FOR CAUTION SIGN #1:**
> All vacations are not what they are cracked up to be! Characters could be a honeymooning couple who lose their wallets, get sunburned, and miss their flight home.

STEP BY STEP

1. Read aloud *The Spider and the Fly* by Tony DiTerlizzi, using a document camera to project the text onto a screen if possible. Call students' attention to the detail in the drawings as they listen. Notice that the spider web that surrounds the dialogue gets thicker and more intricate as the Spider slowly ensnares his prey.
2. Before reading the Spider's letter in the Epilogue, return to the first page, and call on students to take the parts of the Spider and the Fly, while you reads the narration. Remind students that expressive reading increases understanding.
3. During the reading ask:
   - *Is the Spider sincere when he suggests that he will snugly tuck the Fly in for a nap? How do you know?*
   - *What about the Spider's dialogue creates distrust?*
   - *The Fly declines the Spider's attention in words, but do you believe that she will stick to her guns? Why or why not?*
   - *What finally causes the Fly to give in to all the flattery?* (the mirror)
4. Pair up students and distribute the Character Web reproducible. Ask them to decide which student will fill in the Spider Web and which will work on the Fly Web. Invite them to work together to come up with their analysis of each character by following the instructions on the reproducible. Make sure the book is available for reference.
5. Share webs as a class: Explain to the class that a timer will be set for one-minute intervals. Every time they hear the timer go off, the spiders must find a different fly with whom to share web ideas.

WRAP-UP

In reading journals, invite the students to discuss the characteristic qualities of either the Spider or the Fly from one of the author roles described below. As the writer, remind students to consider their purpose as they describe the characters. Their purpose will affect what the reader comes to believe about the characters.

- You are a newspaper reporter, writing a front-page story about the murder of the Fly. Your audience is the readers of the newspaper.
- You are Charlotte (from *Charlotte's Web,* by E. B. White) writing a letter about the importance of honesty. Your cousin, the Spider, is the recipient of the letter.
- You are the Spider (or the Fly) writing a journal entry about your busy day.

LESSON 8

Analyzing Character Traits in Tall Tales

MODEL TEXT

Thunder Rose
Written by Jerdine Nelson
Illustrated by Kadir Nelson
Harcourt, 2003, 32 pp.

In this beautifully illustrated tall tale, readers will meet Miss "Thunder" Rose. Everything that she does, including being born on a stormy night, is done with gusto. She overcomes any and all challenges that come her way. She has remarkable abilities and is able to hold thunder and lightning in her hands, speak in sentences, lift a cow, and lasso clouds. So, when a tornado threatens her community, she uses her power of song to "touch the heart of the clouds."

MATERIALS

- 1 copy of a Paul Bunyan tale
- chart paper
- 1 copy of *Thunder Rose*
- copies of Tall Tale Character Traits (page 59; 1 copy per student)
- copies of Tall Tale Comic Strip Prewrite (page 60; 1 copy per student)
- copies of Tall Tale Comic Strip (page 61; 1 copy per student)

This Coretta Scott King honor book (for illustration) showcases a sassy and energetic character and is perfect for a unit on tall tales and characterization.

CRITICAL QUESTION

How does the reader analyze tall tale character traits?

WARM-UP

Before reading aloud a Paul Bunyan tale, draw two columns on a piece of chart paper and direct students to do the same on a piece of notebook paper. Together, label the left column Exaggerated Traits and the right column Human Traits.

Explain to students that in tall tales characters usually have both exaggerated traits and human traits. Also note that the extraordinary traits are usually physical. For instance, Paul Bunyan is "as strong as ten grizzlies and sixty-three ax handles high." Emphasize that Paul's human traits, such as his cheerful nature and desire for friendship, are often universal.

As students listen to the tale, ask them to list some of Paul's exaggerated and human traits in the appropriate columns. After the reading, have students share their lists. Record their responses on the chart paper.

STEP BY STEP

1. Tell students that they are now going to listen to a tall tale about Thunder Rose, one of the toughest, most heroic cowgirls in the West. Let them know that they should identify Thunder Rose's exaggerated and human traits as they listen to the tale.
2. Begin reading the tale aloud. Stop briefly several times during the story and ask pairs of students to quickly state some of Rose's exaggerated and human traits. Below are some stopping points for you to consider (read to the bottom of each page):
   - page 7
   - page 8
   - page 11
   - page 15
   - page 18
   - page 20
   - page 24
   - page 27
   - page 29
3. After reading, form groups of three. Direct students to number themselves from 1 to 3. Distribute copies of Tall Tale Character Traits.
4. Explain to students that each member of the group will become an expert on one of the quotations. Assign the first quote to the 1s, the second to the 2s, and the third to the 3s.
5. Instruct students to analyze the quote to discover what exaggerated traits and what human traits it reveals. Read and explain the model answer before students begin their analyses. Here are some possible responses:

EXAGGERATED TRAITS:

1. strong enough to bend metal
2. her eyes shoot lightning bolts and her thundering feet crate a violent storm
3. powerful enough to calm tornadoes, produce rain, and end a drought; able to communicate with (affect) clouds

HUMAN TRAITS:

1. compassionate; natural teacher—helps young children learn to read
2. hot tempered; angered by her failure to make it rain and for stirring up the sky, which caused the tornado funnels
3. loving—recognizes the healing, transforming power of love that resides in all human beings

6. Provide time for "experts" to analyze their quotes and to share their responses with group members.
7. Inform group members that they need to evaluate each student's response before recording his/her information on their organizer. If they disagree with someone's answer, they must offer other suggestions and provide evidence to support their interpretation.
8. Afterward, tell students that they will have one minute to share each of their responses with a different partner, someone with whom they have not already worked. Inform students that when you say, "Share," they will quickly find another student and exchange information about quote 1. Explain that when you say, "Swap partners," they are to find a new partner with whom to share. Repeat this process for quotes 2 and 3.

WRAP-UP

Explain to students that they will create a tall-tale character and showcase one deed the character performs.

Distribute copies of the Tall Tale Comic Strip Prewrite and review the directions. Instruct students to complete the organizer before designing their cartoons. When students complete the organizer, they may use the Tall Tale Comic Strip organizer to create their comic.

Direct students to color their final copies. In small groups, have students share their final products and then display the cartoons around the classroom.

More Books for Teaching CHARACTERIZATION

The Boy Who Loved Words
Written by Roni Schotter
Illustrated by Giselle Potter
Schwartz & Wade Books, 2006, 40 pp.

Everyone is a collector of sorts, and the main character of this story is no different. Selig collects words. Whenever he hears a word that he likes, he writes it on a slip of paper and saves it in a convenient place (e.g., a pocket, sock, or hat). His eccentricities do not go unnoticed, and soon he is known as "Wordsworth," which is another word for his collection. Selig's curiosity about words does make him somewhat of an "oddball" until he finds a purpose for his collection, such as leaving words on tree branches so a poet could write about the moon melting like a "lemon lozenge in the licorice sky." Through the act of sharing his words, he discovers his purpose in life. The illustrations reinforce the power of language with slips of paper in various fonts sprinkled across the pages. Another helpful feature is the two-page glossary with an explanation of unfamiliar terms.

TEACHING IDEA

- Discuss how Selig's personality changes throughout the story. Using a sociogram, have students plot the relationships between Selig and the other characters in the story, pointing out their interactions.

INTERDISCIPLINARY CONNECTION

- Invite students to create their own word journals or envelopes to add their favorite words. Words journals can also feature content-specific vocabulary for various subjects.
- Support reading comprehension by having students complete a Cloze Passage such as the one at the top of the following page.

CLOZE PASSAGE FOR *THE BOY WHO LOVED WORDS* (CREATED BY SUSAN VAN ZILE)

Selig ________ everything about words—the sound of them in his ears (tintinnabulating!), the taste of them on his tongue (________ !), the thought of them when they ________ in his brain (stirring!), and, most especially, the feel of them when they moved his heart (Mama!).

Whenever Selig heard a word he liked, he'd ________ it loud, ________ it down on a piece of paper, then ________ it into his pocket to save. Such a collector!

Selig's pockets positively ________ with words. He stuffed new ones inside his ________ , down his ________ , up his ________ , under his ________ .

Doña Flor: A Tall Tale About a Giant Woman With a Great Big Heart

Written by Pat Mora
Illustrated by Raul Colón
Knopf, 2005, 40 pp.

In this Pura Belpré Award-winning book, readers meet Doña Flor, a very tall lady with a huge heart. When Flor was a little girl, her mother sang many songs to her. The songs made the cornstalks grow very healthy and tall; but more important, they made Flor grow extremely tall, too. Flor's height becomes an important gift to her village. She is known as *una amiga* and protector to all, so when she learns that a ferocious animal is terrorizing the villagers, she sets out to find the source. Readers will be surprised to find out who is really making the loud roars. This is an excellent book to use during a tall tale unit and to develop reading comprehension.

TEACHING IDEA

- Discuss Doña Flor's physical traits and how they contribute to her personal character. Ask students to identify the phrases that the author uses to describe her appearance. Encourage students to use words, phrases, and illustrations to learn more about the character.

INTERDISCIPLINARY CONNECTIONS

- Invite students to compare the tall tale of Doña Flor to another one of their favorites.
- Ask students to write and illustrate their own tall tales. If possible, use audio-recording software so students can record their original stories.

Gone With the Wand

Written by Margie Palatini
Illustrated by Brian Ajhar
Orchard Books, 2009, 40 pp.

Bernice Sparklestein, the world's greatest fairy godmother, discovers her wand has lost its magic. Her dear friend Edith B. Cuspid, second class tooth fairy, desperately tries to find Bernice another line of work. After three failed attempts at being a duster, a flaker, and a candygram taker, Bernice becomes despondent. Edith, using a bit of her own magic and deception, helps Bernice discover her true calling as a Goodnight, Sleeptight, Don't Let the Bed Bugs Bite Fairy Godmother. Ajhar's extraordinary caricatures and attention to detail enhance Palatini's puns and make this hilarious tale an unforgettable story about friendship.

TEACHING IDEA

- Create life-sized human outlines on butcher paper and invite students to create their own personal fairy godmother. Be sure to have them identify the characteristics that they would find important, and use their creativity to create an original look.

INTERDISCIPLINARY CONNECTION

- Students can create a Readers Theater script for the book and perform it for an audience. Consider giving students the option to create and use simple props.

Kate and the Beanstalk

Written by Mary Pope Osborne
Illustrated by Giselle Potter
Atheneum Books for Young Readers, 2000, 32 pp.

In this version of the classic tale, a girl named Kate climbs to the top of a beanstalk and outsmarts the giant. Kate is a strong-willed girl who decides to retrieve three precious treasures from the giant when she learns that she is the daughter of a knight that the giant killed. Kate's resourcefulness and wit help her successfully obtain the hen, the gold, and the harp, which rightfully belong to her and her mother. This humorous adaptation of the original story will delight readers of all ages.

TEACHING IDEA

■ Use a character map and ask students to brainstorm the characteristics of Jack from the original tale. Then, ask them to discuss how Kate is similar to or different from Jack. Record the responses on a Venn diagram to help students compare and contrast the two characters. Some questions to pose include: *Do you feel that Kate was smart? Was she smarter than Jack? In what ways?*

INTERDISCIPLINARY CONNECTION

■ In small groups, ask students to draw a body biography of Kate to illustrate her character traits. A body biography is a life-sized visual representation of a character in a story that contains visual and textual representations of the character.

Marven of the Great North Woods

Written by Kathryn Lasky
Illustrated by Kevin Hawkes
Harcourt Brace, 1997, 48 pp.

This historical-fiction picture book introduces readers to ten-year-old Marven, who is sent away from his home to keep him safe from the deadly influenza epidemic. He takes the train to visit a family friend's Minnesota logging camp, where he is given the task of keeping the payroll books for the loggers. He is told that "he's got a head for numbers." During his time at the camp, Marven makes friends with one of the men, Jean Louis. This friendship teaches Marven about the importance of logging. He eventually returns home to find that his family has survived the epidemic. Based on the childhood of author Lasky's father, this Notable Social Studies Trade Books for Young People winner also includes a note about why Marven, and not any of his sisters, was sent away.

TEACHING IDEA

■ Ask students to consider the following questions: *How do the characters feel about each other? How do you know? How do the characters' feelings change? How do you know? What is the role of each character? Why do the characters act the way they do and say the things they say?* Then invite students to write a diary entry or letter to Marven's parents, from Marven's point of view, to describe his friendship with Jean Louis. Be sure to encourage students to write how Marven has changed since his first day at the logging camp.

INTERDISCIPLINARY CONNECTIONS

■ This book serves as an excellent springboard to discuss the life of lumberjacks and the logging process.

■ Compare the differences of the logging process today and of the past and lead students into an inquiry project to learn more information.

My Great-Aunt Arizona

Written by Gloria Houston
Illustrated by Susan Condie Lamb
HarperCollins, 1992, 32 pp.

This beautiful and heartwarming story celebrates teachers and one-room schoolhouses. Born in a log cabin in the Blue Ridge Mountains, Arizona has always dreamed of becoming a teacher. After setting off to college, she has returned home to teach generations of children. She returns to the one-room schoolhouse that she attended, gets married, and even brings her own children to school, but never really goes to any of the "faraway" places that she dreamed about visiting when she was young. Arizona is a strong female protagonist whose stories and infectious personality will remind readers of the past while extending an appreciation for the Appalachian region.

TEACHING IDEA

■ Discuss Arizona's growth as a character from childhood to adulthood. Explore what Arizona likes to do as a girl and what she does after finishing school. Discuss how Arizona exemplifies the characteristics of a strong heroine of her time.

INTERDISCIPLINARY CONNECTIONS

- Read this book during Women's History Month (March) as a springboard for learning more about the many contributions that women have made throughout history.
- Ask students to interview a woman in their life who is especially important to them. Invite students to complete an oral history project for which they will create a picture book including photos, newspaper clippings, quotes, historical artifacts, and so on, in the style of *My Great-Aunt Arizona,* to celebrate the significance of this special individual.

The Odious Ogre

Written by Norton Juster
Illustrated by Jules Feiffer
Michael di Capua/Scholastic, 2010, 32 pp.

The odious ogre has a horrible reputation for being a terrible creature. When he arrives, hungry, at a small and remote cottage, he meets a young girl who has never heard of him. He stomps, roars, and smashes nearby objects, but she is not afraid. Instead, she offers him tea and kind words. The ogre is humiliated and leaves wondering, "How can I live if I can't ravage and plunder?" The gentle humor of this tale is accentuated by Feiffer's warm and expressive illustrations.

TEACHING IDEA

- Discuss all of the descriptive words that the author uses to paint a picture of the ogre's personality and physical traits. Then ask students to identify the ogre's character traits and compose a personality poem (or bio-poem). Here is an example of the template:

> ________________________________,
> (character's name)
> Who is __________, __________, __________.
> (three adjectives that describe the character)
> Who loves __________.
> Who fears __________.
> Who needs __________.
> Who gives __________.
> Who believes __________.
>
> ________________________________
> (character's name)

INTERDISCIPLINARY CONNECTIONS

- This book introduces students to many adjectives and adverbs, so it is a wonderful source to teach vocabulary in context. Ask students to define, illustrate, and use different words in context.
- Ask students to create a comic strip displaying dialogue between the ogre and a new character.

The Princess and the Pizza

Written by Mary Jane Auch
Illustrated by Mary Jane and Herm Auch
Holiday House, 2002, 32 pp.

This Storytelling World Award-winning book is a humorous tale of Princess Paulina's quest to find a prince. Through a series of competitive tasks, Paulina easily passes the old "pea hidden under twelve mattresses" test and other age-old classic tests. The final test involves preparing a meal for the Prince, using only select ingredients of flour, yeast, water, tomatoes, and cheese. As predicted, Paulina becomes the queen of pizza and, in the end, decides not to marry Prince Drupert after all. She returns to her village and opens the pizza shop, where the prince and his mother, Queen Zelda, dine every Thursday. This is a remarkably zany tale full of twists and spoofs accompanied by exaggerated visual illustrations.

TEACHING IDEAS

- Discuss the types of adjectives that the author uses to tell what a character is like (direct characterization). Then, list the verbs that the author uses to show what the character does (indirect characterization).
- Ask students to complete a character-change story map to visually plot how the princess changed her mind about marrying a prince. The story map would include three columns ("character at the beginning"; "events that caused the change"; and "character at the end").

INTERDISCIPLINARY CONNECTIONS

- Learn more about the history of pizza. Students can also check out the pizza world records to learn about the world's largest pizza and the world's largest pizza order.

■ This picture book works well for exploring point of view. Students can write another version from Prince Drupert's point of view or one of the other princesses.

■ Invite students to write a letter to Queen Zelda telling her what qualities are needed to make a perfect princess.

Scoop! An Exclusive

Written by Monty Molenski
Additional words and pictures by John Kelly and Cathy Tincknell
Candlewick, 2007, 32 pp.

In this visually appealing book, mole reporter Monty Molenski is trying to make an impression on his editor. So, he needs an appealing story to make the front page. Monty overhears some of his colleagues talking about a meeting at the F. P. Club and sneaks into the building only to discover that F. P. means writers who have made the front page. Throughout his journey, his camera accidentally flashes and the developed pictures reveal a potential story. Readers will "scoop" up this appealing story of Monty Molenski's adventure.

TEACHING IDEA

■ Have students complete a Frayer Model about Monty Molenski. A Frayer Model is a word categorization activity that helps learners develop their understanding of various concepts (Frayer, et al., 1969). In this case, prepare a visual of the model by dividing a sheet of paper into four sections, with the character's name in the center. Place the following prompts in the quadrants:

- What makes this character admirable?
- How did this character respond to conflict? Provide details from the story.
- What are some adjectives and/or character traits to describe the character?
- Describe a lesson that you learned from the character.

INTERDISCIPLINARY CONNECTIONS

■ The visual layout of this picture book makes it a model text to experiment with using Web 2.0 technologies to produce student writing.

■ Invite students to create a comic strip about Monty's next adventure or work together in groups to prepare a front-page news story.

Show Way

Written by Jacqueline Woodson
Illustrated by Hudson Talbott
G. P. Putnam's Sons, 2005, 48 pp.

Based on the author's own family, this award-winning selection tells the story of African-American women across seven generations, from slavery to freedom, through segregation, freedom marches, and the struggle for literacy and social justice. A "show way" is a quilt with secret meanings to show escaping slaves the way to safety. The multimedia art adds to the overall themes of love and courage.

TEACHING IDEA

■ In this story, the author shares her own story through personal narrative employing free verse. The symbolism that is woven throughout adds depth and meaning, while the stories depict characters with common traits. Invite students to chart the change in characters and how these changes empowered courage and enabled freedom.

INTERDISCIPLINARY CONNECTIONS

■ Help students understand symbolism while identifying character traits through art. Ask students to create symbolic representations of themselves or of someone who is special to them. Using art materials, students will create symbols and also include quotes to share while discussing their personal character traits with a small group.

■ Encourage students to make their own story quilt square and identify the most important skill(s) that their mother or other female role model in their family has taught them.

■ The book explores the powerful theme of finding our heritage through family stories and artifacts, which provide a mirror to the past and a window to the future. This book is an excellent addition to a text set about the role of quilts in history.

Weslandia

Written by Paul Fleischman
Illustrated by Kevin Hawkes
Candlewick, 1999, 40 pp.

This Notable Children's Books in the Language Arts selection tells the story of a young man named Wesley. His unique personality and quirkiness lead him to devise a most unusual summer project. He decides to create a brand new civilization built around a mysterious crop grown from seeds blown in by the westward wind. This garden defines Wesley's amicable qualities and natural creativity. Through descriptive language and delightful illustrations, readers learn that Wesley is different from the other kids and that, through his imagination, he not only creates a summer hideout but also has formed a few new friendships.

TEACHING IDEA

- Discuss the actions of the main character (Wesley) and how his enterprising attributes led him to create his own civilization. Then ask students to work with a partner to complete a character report card for Wesley. How would they evaluate Wesley in the following areas: Creativity; Intelligence; Uniqueness; Bravery; Athleticism?

INTERDISCIPLINARY CONNECTIONS

- Invite students to create their own special land. They can use their name, as Wesley did (i.e., Susanlandia or Emilylandia). Students can create an interactive poster online, using a site such as Glogster to visually represent their new world and share their adventure stories with the class.
- Instruct students to write a letter using a RAFT (Santa, 1988), which is an acronym that stands for Role, Audience, Format, and Topic. It is a system to guide students to understand their role as a writer, the audience that they will address, the various formats used in writing, and the expected content. In the case of the story, students can pretend that Wesley (Role) is writing a letter to his distant uncle (Audience) in an e-mail (Format) and wants to share his counting system and how it works (Topic). Another example is to pretend that one of Wesley's schoolmates (Role) wants to invite Wesley (Audience) to a birthday party (Format is the invitation), and includes the reasons he should attend (Topic).

Willy the Wimp

Written and illustrated by Anthony Browne
Knopf/Random House, 1984, 32 pp.

Readers will meet Willy, a kind and gentle chimpanzee who is bullied by the suburban gorilla gang. He is ridiculed and called names, such as "Willy the Wimp." Desperate to do something about his situation, Willy answers a body-building advertisement in a popular magazine. After following this plan, he grows big and strong and saves Millie from being mugged. Everything seems to be going well for Willy, and it looks like things are set to change, even for a little while. Anthony Browne's surrealistic illustrations and storylines will delight readers.

TEACHING IDEAS

- Willy undertook both physical and emotional changes in the story. Ask students to compose a script that dramatizes the changes that Willy experiences.
- Suggest that students create a visual representation to show the changes that take place with Willy.

INTERDISCIPLINARY CONNECTIONS

- Ask students to research more information about chimpanzees and gorillas.
- Read and discuss other books written by Anthony Browne. Then, ask students to write a personal response to the texts, comparing the characters, symbolism, themes, and so on.
- Consider having students listen to a Web interview of Anthony Browne to learn more about his artistic style. Guide them in a discussion about how Browne uses slapstick humor, both in his writing and with visual clues, to illustrate Willy's character.

CAUTIONARY TALES

Name: ______________________________

Underneath each of the caution signs, identify a warning about which the author could be writing, and name two possible characters that could be used to give the warning in a story. Let your imagination go! In the last sign, create your own caution!

____

____

____

____

____

____

____

____

____

____

____

____

CHARACTER WEB

Name: ______________________________

In the three rectangles around the word "Spider" or "Fly" write one word or quality that describes that character. In the other spaces, describe dialogue in the story that supports each quality you listed. For example: The Spider is a flatterer. The story moment that supports this is when the Spider tells the Fly that she has beautiful eyes.

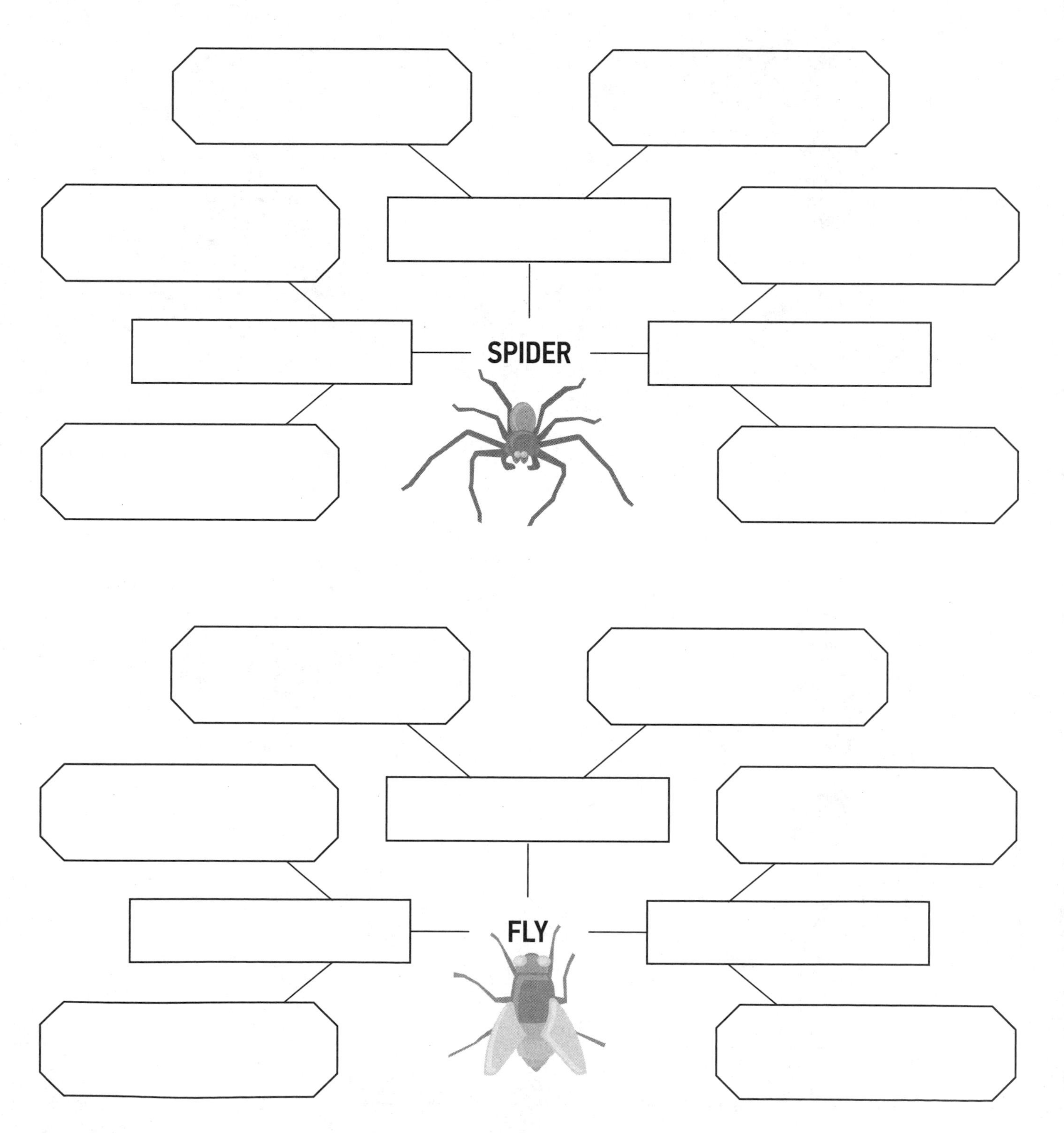

TALL TALE CHARACTER TRAITS

Name: ____________________

To discover some of Thunder Rose's character traits, analyze the quote you have been assigned. Use the model below and what you know about Rose to guide your thinking. Record your response in the appropriate box.

THE TEXT	EXAGGERATED TRAITS Thunder Rose is . . .	HUMAN TRAITS Rose is . . .
"She was as pretty as a picture, had the sweetest disposition, but don't let yourself be misled, that child was full of thunder and lightning." (page 11)	loud as thunder and as powerful as lightning	gorgeous, kind, and very sweet
1. "By the time she turned twelve, Rose had perfected her metal-bending practices. She formed delicately shaped alphabet letters to help young ones learn to read." (page 14)		
2. "Oh this riled Rose so much, she became the only two-legged tempest to walk the western plains . . . . Her eyes flashed lightning." (page 24)		
3. "And, gentle as a baby's bath, a soft, drenching-and-soaking rain fell. And Rose realized that by reaching into her own heart to bring forth the music that was there, she had even touched the hearts of the clouds." (page 28)		

TALL TALE COMIC STRIP PREWRITE

Name: ______________________________

Use the organizer below to plan your comic strip. Develop an original tall tale character. Name your character and list some of his or her exaggerated traits. Decide on one superhuman deed your character will perform.

CHARACTER'S NAME ______________________________

EXAGGERATED TRAITS/ABILITIES

____

____

____

HUMAN TRAITS

____

____

____

DEED PERFORMED

____

____

____

TALL TALE COMIC STRIP

Name: ____________________

Use your Tall Tale Comic Strip Prewrite to help you create an original tall tale comic strip in the boxes below.
Color and display your work.

CHAPTER 5 • THEME

"Walking home from school, I knew how he felt, how lonely he must be. Maybe I should have said something to those mean kids."

—from *Wings* (page 24)

Theme refers to the main idea or underlying meaning of a literary work. A story can have more than one theme and it can be implied or transparent. Readers need to distinguish the difference between the theme and the topic of a literary work. For example, if the topic of a literary work is bullying, then the theme may be the idea that bullying is harmful and that individuals must respect the differences of others.

The following are two ways through which an author can convey theme in his or her work.

- Affecting the readers' feelings. Readers can explore text-to-self connections and ask themselves what the main character learns during the course of the story.
- Using repeated words and phrases. Readers can look for repeated words and phrases within a character's thoughts or in conversations between characters.

It is important to note that topics such as friendship, loss, or acceptance are different than theme. Topics can be described using one or two words. Themes, on the other hand, are expressed in complete sentences. For example, "Accepting and celebrating personal differences creates a strong community" is a theme. There are many outstanding picture books to demonstrate the literary element of theme. One such example is *Wings*, written and illustrated by Christopher Myers. Through the juxtaposition of text and illustrations, the author sends a powerful and positive message to encourage students to feel worthwhile and valuable. Moreover, throughout the story, the issue of bullying is presented and the main character learns to celebrate his uniqueness.

LESSON 9

Connecting the Title to the Theme

MODEL TEXT

The Junkyard Wonders

Written and illustrated by Patricia Polacco

Philomel Books, 2010, 48 pp.

Based on the author's own childhood experience, this realistic fiction picture book will affirm the special qualities that each child brings to the classroom. Trisha, the main character, is heartbroken to be placed in Miss Peterson's special education class (also known as "the junkyard"), but everyone in this class is treated with respect. More importantly, everyone is encouraged to share their unique talents. This is a heartwarming story that will foster classroom community, diversity, and respect for others.

MATERIALS

- 1 copy of *The Junkyard Wonders*
- picture of a junkyard
- copies of Scraps of Wonder (page 70; 1 copy per student and a transparency or scanned copy to project onto a screen)

CRITICAL QUESTION

How does the author use the title to convey the theme?

WARM-UP

Find an image of a junkyard and show it to the class. As students view the image, tell them that they will listen to a story called *The Junkyard Wonders*. Ask students to explain the meaning of the title as it relates to both the picture and what they know about junkyards. In what sense can a junkyard contain wonders?

STEP BY STEP

1. Distribute the Scraps of Wonder activity page. Instruct students to write down information from the text that relates to the title of the story as they listen.
2. Using a document camera, project a copy of the text onto a screen or hold the book open for all to see. Begin reading.
3. Stop at the bottom of page 8. Ask students what Mrs. Peterson means when she says, "Welcome to the junkyard" (page 8). According to Mrs. Peterson, what fills her junkyard?
4. Project an overhead transparency or a scanned copy of Scraps of Wonder onto a screen. Next to the first piece of junk, write down the insights students offer into this first reference to the junkyard. Direct students to record these notes.
5. Next, read to the bottom of page 10. Partner students. Ask them to discuss what new information they discover about the junkyard and to record their thoughts in the next box on their organizer.
6. Continue reading, stopping at the bottom of pages 21, 22, 23, and 32 to provide time for partners to discuss what these pages reveal about the meaning of the title.
7. Ask partners to examine the evidence from the text they have collected on their graphic organizers to create a theme statement related to the title. Remind students that theme statements are general messages about life.
8. As a class, discuss students' insights into the themes the title conveys. Then ask volunteers to share some of their theme statements. Students may come up with themes such as "everyone deserves respect" or "dreams are achieved through perseverance." If students have difficulty generating theme statements provide more whole-class practice.

WRAP-UP

Ask students to find a piece of junk at home and to transform it into a "wonder." Instruct them to write a theme statement about *The Junkyard Wonders* on an index card and glue it to their invention. Display the inventions and send students on a museum walk to view the new products and various themes. Consider having a Museum Theme Night, and invite parents and community members for a tour of the inventions.

LESSON 10

The Many Colors of Theme

MODEL TEXT

Night Boat to Freedom
Written by Margot Theis Raven
Illustrated by E. B. Lewis
Farrar, Straus and Giroux, 2006, 40 pp.

This Notable Books for a Global Society and Jane Addams Children's Book Award winner draws upon accounts in the Federal Writers' Project Slave Narrative Collection. Twelve-year-old Christmas John lives with his Granny Judith, who was captured as a child in Africa. One evening, Granny Judith asks Christmas John to row a young slave across the river to freedom in Ohio. Even though he is afraid, he perseveres and helps many slaves escape. With each trip, Granny Judith adds a square to the quilt she is making for their trip for freedom. E. B. Lewis's illustrations capture the emotional connection between the two characters.

CRITICAL QUESTION

How are themes revealed in symbols as well as in direct statements by the author?

MATERIALS

- 1 copy of *Night Boat to Freedom*
- a list of color meanings to display (see the sample chart, at right)
- copies of Color Poem 1 (page 71; 1 copy per student)
- copies of Color Poem 2 (page 72; 1 copy per student)
- copies of Double-Sided Notes (page 73; 1 copy per student)
- construction paper cut into 8-inch squares, with two holes punched on each side
- markers and art supplies
- strands of yarn for connecting the quilt squares

COLOR	SYMBOLIZES
red	life, passion, emotion, danger, fire
black	death, ignorance, evil, cold, night
white	innocence, life, purity, enlightenment
green	inexperience, hope, spring, plant life, immaturity
yellow	decay, violence, old age, heat
blue	calm, cool, peace, sky
pink	innocence, femininity
purple	royalty, bruising or pain
brown	earth, humility, poverty

WARM-UP

Explain to students that while "topic" is the best starting point for understanding the "theme" of a literary work, symbols that the author weaves into the story also lead the reader to discover the important big idea that the author wants to convey. A symbol may appear in a work of literature in a number of different ways to suggest a theme. One commonly used symbol is color.

Over time, certain colors have become conventional symbols, and readers can expect them to have classic meaning. Share with students a list of color meanings and ask them for a show of hands if the meanings are familiar. After looking over with students the chart of color meanings, explain that every author can infuse color with his or her own meaning with the intention of creating a theme.

In order to experience this, invite the class to create a color poem and infuse their favorite color with meaning through the poem, thereby creating a theme. Pass out the Color Poem activity pages, which provide students with two choices of format for the color poems. (An Internet search for color poem formats will yield many more choices.)

Find a vehicle for publishing their work. Consider sharing the poems through blogs, a bulletin board, or a class booklet.

STEP BY STEP

1. Transition into the lesson for *Night Boat to Freedom* by holding up the book and informing students that author Margot Theis Raven has infused her story with color symbolism. She has also clearly and directly stated her theme through the dialogue of her characters and the statements of the narrator.
2. Distribute Double-Sided Notes and instruct students to jot down notes about theme under the appropriate columns on the page. If they detect a reference to theme through color, tell students to make a note in the Color Symbolism column. If they hear a directly stated theme, instruct students to make a note in the Direct Statement column.
3. Explain that although this story is fiction, it was inspired by the real life experience of Arnold Gragston. (For the story of his life visit www.menare.org.)
4. Using a document camera, or holding the book open, read the story to the class.
5. Pause at the bottom of the pages indicated to check student responses for theme as well as for references to color significance:

PAGE 6: "turkey red, the color that stole Granny Judith from Africa and put her in slavery . . ."

PAGE 12: "What scares the head is best done with the heart."

PAGE 17: "I remembered to ask Molly what color dress she was wearin'. 'Blue' came back her whispered answer."

PAGE 18: "Night after night it kept me and my secret safe."

"What color is freedom tonight, Christmas John?"

PAGE 21: ". . . we got to get ourselves over the river, 'cause danger's gonna grow awful."

PAGE 25: Turkey red becomes John's freedom color.

PAGE 26: "'cause love don't stop at a river, and no river's wide enough to keep us apart."

PAGE 31: "What scares the head is best done with the heart." (Ask students how the meaning of this quote may have changed since its first appearance.)

WRAP-UP

After finishing the reading, call on several students to share a favorite moment in the story, and ask each one to connect that moment to any ideas he or she has about the theme.

Explain that in the crafting of her quilt, Grandma Judith makes it clear that the color of freedom is different for every person. Then tell students that they will create a visual representation of the theme of this book.

Walk around the room with 8-inch squares of colored construction paper, and ask each student to select his or her own personal color of freedom.

Invite them to write on their square a theme statement about freedom and then decorate the square as a patch for a class quilt. Give students plenty of time to work and a variety of materials to use.

When the squares are completed, ask groups of four to share their squares. Hand each group strands of yarn to lace the four squares together. Then move together two groups of four for more sharing and lacing, until the quilt is complete and can be hung on a wall or bulletin board.

More Books for Teaching THEME

The Bee Tree

Written by Stephen Buchmann and Diana Cohn
Illustrated by Paul Mirocha
Cinco Puntos Press, 2007, 40 pp.

This Skipping Stones Honor Award–winning book is set in the rainforests of Malaysia. A young boy, Nizam, tells the story of how he learned about harvesting honey from the giant tualang tree from his grandfather. It is now Nizam's responsibility to maintain the traditional art of harvesting honey. He must make the 120-foot climb to the bee hives with great care so as not to upset the ecosystem that supports the honey bees. Throughout the story, Nizam shares the legends of bee collectors before him. The themes of courage, ecology, coming of age, preservation and honor are interwoven throughout this story.

TEACHING IDEA

- Invite students to indicate the significance of the theme to the well-being of the village. Ask students to write memories or poems about one of their relatives or grandparents that would capture the essence of their relationship and the theme of family.

INTERDISCIPLINARY CONNECTIONS

- This is an excellent book to incorporate into a unit about honey bees and harvesting or a springboard to discussing the Malaysian rainforest.
- Invite students to compare and contrast the themes in this story with *The Best Beekeeper of Lalibela: A Tale From Africa* by Cristina Kessler and *The Bee Tree* by Patricia Polacco.

Brothers in Hope: The Story of the Lost Boys of Sudan

Written by Mary Williams
Illustrated by R. Gregory Christie
Lee & Low, 2005, 40 pp.

This award-winning book tells the story of Garang, an eight-year old boy living in Sudan. He is tending his family's cattle when his entire village is attacked, destroying his house, his belongings, and his family. He has nowhere left to go except to walk to the next village. On his journey, he meets other boys who have lost their families. They form an alliance to survive and protect each other. They find shelter in refugee camps, but many other refugees die along the way. They travel nearly 1,000 miles across the border, first to Ethiopia, and later to Kenya. This book is based on real-life events and personal stories, and the author founded the Lost Boys Foundation, an organization devoted to helping the real-life "Garangs" in America.

TEACHING IDEA

- Since the title contains a clue that relates to the theme of the work, invite students to discuss their ideas. Ask students to brainstorm what they think "Brothers in Hope" means and why the author decided to share her feelings about this issue.

INTERDISCIPLINARY CONNECTIONS

- Invite students to do some research about Sudan and refugees, and then prepare an interactive poster or other type of presentation about their findings.
- The author uses many similes throughout the book. Draw from the examples to teach a mini-lesson on how students can use similes in their own writing. Examples from the book include: "I could hear bangs like thunder," and "Rushing water roared like an angry lion."

Christmas in the Trenches

Written by John McCutcheon
Illustrated by Henri Sørensen
Peachtree, 2006, 32 pp.

This historical-fiction picture book received multiple honors, including the Notable Social Studies Trade Books for Young People and Notable Books for a Global Society awards. The story begins when Grandpa tells his grandchildren, Thomas and Nora, about his unforgettable Christmas as a young soldier during World War I. Inspired by an actual incident, the story shares how the British soldiers heard the German soldiers singing a familiar tune, "Silent Night," and decided to join them. During the evening, they ate together and even played soccer, but the next day, they fought each other again as if the events of Christmas Eve had never happened. The end matter includes historical notes and a CD with narrations in both English and German.

TEACHING IDEA

- Since the author is also a folk singer/musician, students can discuss that music is a central part of the story's theme. Invite students to discuss the author's view of the "human condition" and how the author communicates his viewpoint.

INTERDISCIPLINARY CONNECTION

- This picture book is essential to include in a text set about World War I or about war in general. It would also work as part of a study of point of view; students can write a letter home from the point of view of a soldier involved in the fighting.

Circle Unbroken: The Story of a Basket and Its People

Written by Margot Theis Raven
Illustrated by E. B. Lewis
Farrar, Straus and Giroux, 2004, 48 pp.

This Notable Books for a Global Society Award–winning book celebrates the Gullah culture in its tradition of sweet-grass basket making and storytelling. The lyrical narrative begins with rites of passage between a grandmother and her granddaughter that surround the basket-weaving tradition from their native Africa. The grandmother demonstrates the unbroken circle of family and ancestors as they dealt with difficult times. Included in the back matter are additional information about sweet-grass baskets and a bibliography of further reading material.

TEACHING IDEA

- Invite students to make a basket using paper strips and include drawings and/or photos to illustrate the themes of the story. Ask students to describe how the author uses the grandmother to express the overall message of the story. Also, ask students to discuss the link between the title and the theme.

INTERDISCIPLINARY CONNECTIONS

- Use this book during a unit about slavery. Arrange to have the class work with the art teacher to explore the historic significance of basket weaving.
- Integrate this story during writing workshop to invite students to linger on the poetic phrases that are used throughout the text to describe the characters and the baskets.

14 Cows for America

Written by Carmen Agra Deedy in collaboration with Wilson Kimeli Naiyomah
Illustrated by Thomas Gonzalez
Peachtree Publishers, 2009, 32 pp.

Kimeli Naiyomah, was a college student from Africa, when he witnessed the destruction of the World Trade Center towers on 9/11, and described the tragedy to his Maasai tribe. The village responded by presenting the American people with a special gift of 14 cows. It is important to understand that to the Maasai people, the cow resembles "life." Within the pages of this story, the written word and the dramatic illustrations pay tribute to the tribe's generosity and compassion.

TEACHING IDEA

- The themes of compassion and generosity are explicit in this selection. Invite students to write about the significance of the theme for humankind.

INTERDISCIPLINARY CONNECTIONS

- This selection will effectively launch conversations about the events of September 11th as well as a unit about African culture.
- Students can conduct inquiry projects to learn more about the Maasai tribe.
- Invite students to compose an original cinquain poem describing what that they learned from the story.

Freedom on the Menu: The Greensboro Sit-Ins

Written by Carole Boston Weatherford
Illustrated by Jerome Lagarrigue
Dial Books for Young Readers, 2005, 32 pp.

This historical-fiction picture book is set in Greensboro, North Carolina, during 1960s and shares the story of desegregation from the viewpoint of one little girl. Connie is a young black girl who explains her experiences of not being allowed to drink from the water fountains or eat in the dining areas that are designated for whites. The focus of the story explores the sit-ins that took place during this time period. For example, in the story, the author describes the time that a group of college students decided to stand up for what they believed to be fair and sit in at the local store. This rise for justice began to spread around the country and led to Connie's siblings participating in the Greensboro sit-ins. This moving story pays tribute to the many peaceful protestors who made a difference by standing up against injustice.

TEACHING IDEA

- Ask students to discuss the link between the title and the overall message of the book. Invite them to write a slogan or create a sign that a protestor could have carried on the picket line during the sit-ins.

INTERDISCIPLINARY CONNECTIONS

- Use this book during a unit on the civil rights movement.
- Ask students to compose a diary from one of the characters' points of view to express the point of the sit-ins, or the theme of the story.

The Greatest Skating Race: A World War II Story From the Netherlands

Written by Louise Borden
Illustrated by Niki Daly
Margaret K. McElderry Books, 2004, 48 pp.

The Greatest Skating Race speaks of courage, strength, and tradition. In this historical-fiction selection, a young Dutch boy dreams of competing in the famous Elfstedentocht, 200-kilometer skating race. He emulates a national skating hero and conducts his own great skating race that allows him to help two children cross the border to Belgium by skating with them to safety along the canals of Holland.

TEACHING IDEA

- Ask students to consider how the main character, Piet Janssen, demonstrated courage and strength. Also invite them to think about what they learned from the characters' actions.

INTERDISCIPLINARY CONNECTION

- This selection is an ideal book to integrate into a text set about World War II. Students can learn more about the Netherlands and also write their own stories about survival and courage.

The Keeping Quilt

Written and illustrated by Patricia Polacco
Simon & Schuster, 1988, 32 pp.

In this beautifully illustrated story, a quilt is passed along from generation to generation. The quilt is carefully made from the clothing of family members who immigrated to the United States. Throughout the story, Patricia discusses how the cloth was used as a Sabbath tablecloth, a wedding canopy, and as a blanket to welcome each new child into the world.

TEACHING IDEA

- Ask students to make a quilt square that illustrates the themes of the story and includes one item of significance to their lives.

INTERDISCIPLINARY CONNECTION

- Invite students to write a memoir about family customs. Using a quilt graphic organizer, ask students to brainstorm all of the traditions that make their family special. Have them create a final project that best exemplifies their memories (e.g., interactive poster, podcast, book, scrapbook, poetry).

The School Is Not White!: A True Story of the Civil Rights Movement

Written by Doreen Rappaport
Illustrated by Curtis James
Hyperion Books for Children, 2005, 40 pp.

This is a true story about the Carter family and their struggle to integrate their children into the all-white school in Drew, Mississippi, in 1965. Mae Bertha and Matthew Carter enrolled their children in the school despite violent threats. Although it was a struggle, the Carter children did attend the school, where they faced insults from other students. Despite all of these obstacles, the family demonstrated courage and perseverance. The author carefully weaves facts and dialogue to impart the courage and determination of the family. The back matter includes information about how education affected the life of each Carter child.

TEACHING IDEA

- Ask students to brainstorm their thoughts and feelings as they listen to the text and write down examples of situations where they experienced prejudice or the desire to give up because of discouraging situations or words. Encourage students to consider how the author conveys the theme of courage throughout the selection.

INTERDISCIPLINARY CONNECTIONS

- This story fits perfectly in a text set about the civil rights movement.
- Students can also create a time line of the Carter family and compare it to the history of the public education system.

Wings

Written and illustrated by Christopher Myers
Scholastic, 2000, 40 pp.

In this Charlotte Zolotow Honor Award book, author/illustrator Myers retells the myth of Icarus through the voice of Ikarus Jackson. Ikarus, a new boy in the neighborhood, can fly above the rooftops and over a crowd. The winged character nearly falls from the sky—not because he flies too high, but because children in the schoolyard taunt him for being different. The narrator of this story happens to be a shy girl, with a resilient and sensitive disposition, and she empathizes with Ikarus. She provides words of encouragement and helps to rebuild Ikarus's soaring spirit. As indicated by the author, the theme of this book is simple: "Every child has his own beauty and her own talents." The book is suitable for building tolerance and respect for everyone in a community of learners and beyond.

TEACHING IDEAS

- Invite students to write about their own special talents and qualities.
- Conduct a grand conversation about the theme of the book. Invite students to consider how the narrator made a positive impact on the character's life. Encourage students to consider how they may have had an effect on another person's life, whether it be helping someone pick up his or her own books in the hallway, holding the door open for someone, or paying someone a compliment.

INTERDISCIPLINARY CONNECTIONS

- As Linda Christensen states, "Students write more authentically and powerfully when they write pieces about what they care about" (page 213); therefore, provide students with opportunities to write poems about their heritage (e.g., "Where I'm From") and to become active members of the school community by considering how to be more accepting of others.
- Visit the following websites for excellent ideas about integrating social justice and tolerance within the classroom community:

www.tolerance.org

www.literacyforsocialjustice.com/resources

SCRAPS OF WONDER

Name: ______________________________

Each time your teacher comes to a stopping point in *The Junkyard Wonders,* think about how the information in the text relates to the title of the book and the theme of the story. Record your ideas in the boxes with each piece of "junk." Afterward, review your responses and use them to help you write a theme statement that expresses the title's meaning.

THEME STATEMENT: ______________________________

____

COLOR POEM 1

Name: ____________________

Fill in the writing frame below to create one type of color poem. Study the example to help you understand this format.

Name a color: ____________________

Name three things that are that color: ____________________

____

____

Name three things that sound like the color: ____________________

____

____

Name three things that taste like the color: ____________________

____

____

Name three things that feel like the color: ____________________

____

____

What can your color do? ____________________

____

EXAMPLE

RED

A bunch of roses,

The flush of cold cheeks,

A glow of a smoldering fire.

The sound of a trumpet playing jazz,

A horn honking in traffic,

The roar of a jet lifting up into the air.

Watermelon on a hot day,

Chili with extra jalapeños,

Cinnamon hearts on Valentine's Day.

A velvet-covered cushion,

Finger paint on that special paper,

The chill up my spine when I hear the crack of lightning.

Red will take you for a ride, and then break your sweet little heart.

COLOR POEM 2

Name: ____________________

Fill in the writing frame below to create one type of color poem. Study the example to help you understand this format. For this color poem, you may use the same color throughout the poem or try different colors for each verse.

Have you heard the sound of ____________________?

If not, then . . .

Can you hear ____________________?

Can you hear ____________________?

Can you hear ____________________?

If you can . . .

You have heard the sound of ____________________.

Have you tasted the flavor of ____________________?

If not, then . . .

Can you taste ____________________?

Can you taste ____________________?

Can you taste ____________________?

If you can . . .

You have tasted the flavor of ____________________.

Have you smelled the scent of ____________________?

If not, then . . .

Can you smell ____________________?

Can you smell ____________________?

Can you smell ____________________?

If you can . . .

You have smelled the scent of ____________________.

Have you seen the beauty of ____________________?

If not, then . . .

Can you see ____________________?

Can you see ____________________?

Can you see ____________________?

If you can . . .

You have seen the beauty of ____________________.

EXAMPLE

Have you heard the sound of forest green?

If not, then . . .

Can you hear the sadness of a funeral?

Can you hear the presence of your best friend?

Can you hear the sweetness of a sleeping baby?

If you can . . .

You have heard the sound of forest green.

DOUBLE-SIDED NOTES

Name: ____

As your teacher reads aloud *Night Boat to Freedom*, think about what you have learned about theme. Remember that the theme can be revealed through symbols as well as through the feelings and actions of characters. It can also be directly stated in narration and dialogue. Jot down moments in the story when you make a connection to the theme through color symbolism or detect a direct statement of theme. You will use these notes to craft a theme statement after listening to the story.

COLOR SYMBOLISM	DIRECT STATEMENT

THEME STATEMENT: ____

____

CHAPTER 6 • FORESHADOWING

"'Do you see those leaves blowing in the wind? They are torn from the trees like slave children are torn from their families.'"

—from *Henry's Freedom Box* (page 4)

Foreshadowing is the author's use of clues to hint at what might happen later in the story. Writers use foreshadowing to build their readers' expectations and to create suspense. It adds dramatic tension to a story by creating anticipation about what might happen next.

Henry's Freedom Box, by Ellen Levine, is one excellent example of text to use to introduce students to foreshadowing because it provides both verbal and visual clues that foreshadow major events in the story.

To identify examples of foreshadowing in a text, encourage students to:

- be aware of details that are unusual or have emotional significance
- look for phrases that appear to relate to the future
- observe changes in the mood or setting
- identify objects that appear to have a symbolic connection to the story
- notice foreboding statements the narrator or other characters make

By recognizing and understanding foreshadowing, readers can make better predictions while enhancing their comprehension of the material.

LESSON 11

Foreshadowing in Four Voices

MATERIALS

- 1 copy of *Voices in the Park*
- copies of Foreshadowing in Four Voices (1 copy per student; page 83)

MODEL TEXT

Voices in the Park

Written and illustrated by Anthony Browne
DK Publishing, 1998, 32 pp.

At first glance, this is a simple story about a day in the park. But a careful reading reveals one event told from the perspective of four different visitors to the park, on the same day and during the same moments. A snobbish and well-off mother brings her shy son and pedigreed dog to the park at the same time an unemployed father brings his outgoing daughter and playful mutt for an afternoon of fun. The first character to speak foreshadows the thoughts and actions of the consecutive characters. The details in the artwork of Anthony Browne partner with his text to reflect each character's unique point of view as well as to foreshadow events to come.

CRITICAL QUESTION

How does a reader analyze foreshadowing in both the text and illustrations of a picture book?

WARM-UP

Ask the class to think about superheroes they know who transform from ordinary individuals into extraordinary human beings. Brainstorm a list of superheroes with whom the class is familiar, such as Superman, Spiderman, or Batman.

As a class or in small groups, have students generate a list of clues people might be able to use to discover the hidden identity of the superhero. For example, Clark Kent always disappears when a crisis erupts. Also, without his glasses, his face looks exactly like Superman's.

After the class finishes creating the list of clues, explain that these are examples of foreshadowing, a device authors and movie producers use to provide hints or clues about what will happen later in the story. In this case, the clues are related to the character's transformation, which occurs when a dangerous situation or event arises.

STEP BY STEP

1. Explain to students that many authors, like the creators of superhero comic books, use foreshadowing to provide clues to future events in a story. Tell students that often foreshadowing comes at the beginning of a text. Note that details in both the writing and illustrations can foreshadow events to come.
2. Before reading aloud *Voices in the Park*, tell students that the story is written in four parts. In each section, a different narrator provides his or her version of the same event, a walk in the park. Direct students to pay careful attention to the illustrations, because they include many examples of foreshadowing.
3. Project a copy of the front cover onto a screen, using a document camera, or hold the book up for students to see. Ask: *What do you observe about the two characters pictured? What does the boy have in his hand? What kind of relationship does he seem to have with the girl? How is the relationship between the boy and the girl mirrored in the relationship between the two dogs?*
4. Read aloud to students the "First Voice" section. After reading, distribute copies of Foreshadowing in Four Voices. Together, identify the examples of foreshadowing and the events foreshadowed.

Examples of possible responses appear below.

SECTION OF TEXT	EXAMPLES OF FORESHADOWING	EVENT FORESHADOWED
First Voice	the calling trees	the mother calling her son
	Victoria's disappearance	Charles's disappearance
	the pedigree dog meets the mongrel	rich, well-groomed Charles meets the rough-looking child

5. Pair up students. Continue the process of reading and stopping after each of the four sections. After each stopping point, have the partners collect and record the examples of foreshadowing and the related events on their graphic organizer.
6. After finishing the story, direct each pair of students to share one clue and one event with the entire class.

WRAP-UP

Have the class brainstorm a new voice to add to the story, such as Victoria's or Albert's. Remind students to consider less obvious possibilities, such as the homeless Santa, the mother's hat, or the flying statue.

Instruct students to choose one of the voices from the list and use it to create another "chapter" of the story titled "Fifth Voice." Direct students to include examples of foreshadowing in the text.

Emphasize that students will need to consider both the setting and the personality of the characters to create foreshadowing that fits the tone of the book. Remind students about the importance of word choice and emotion in developing foreshadowing.

Encourage students to illustrate their text. As students share their "Fifth Voice" in small groups, ask the listeners to identify examples of foreshadowing. Then post the stories around the room.

LESSON 12

Using Repetition and Rhyme to Foreshadow

MODEL TEXT

The Follower
Written by Richard Thompson
Illustrated by Martin Springett
Fitzhenry & Whiteside, 2000, 32 pp.

In this haunting and mysterious story, something is following a witch home each night. She walks through twisted forests, past creepy statues, and through torrential storms; always followed by "It." The sinister and dark illustrations provide the reader with the clues before the witch solves the mystery for herself. Repetition of pattern and careful rhyme create suspense and foreshadow the ending, by building upon each page with an added detail describing the witch's journey home. The mood, created by the gray and cold illustrations, does not lighten until the end, when the witch invites the cat into a warm and cozy home.

CRITICAL QUESTION

How does the use of repetition build suspense and foreshadow the ending in a story or a poem?

WARM-UP

Remind students that foreshadowing is a technique that authors use to create suspense and build anticipation. Foreshadowing invites the reader to think about what will happen next. In poems and in stories told in verse, the author uses poetic devices such as rhyme and repetition to foreshadow. It sets up expectations for the reader that are fulfilled or frustrated (and often *both* fulfilled and frustrated). In addition, a change in the repetition can indicate a surprise ending.

To illustrate this idea, pass out the lyrics to "The Old Lady Who Swallowed the Fly." Distribute to students copies of Rhyme, Repetition, and Foreshadowing. In small groups or with a partner ask students to use the graphic organizer to identify the features of this childhood rhyme.

Ask students if they know of other examples in which an ending is foreshadowed by building on previous verses. ("Twelve Days of Christmas" is one that might come to mind.) Instruct them to keep this device in mind as you read a more complex yet similarly structured poem.

MATERIALS

- copies of "The Old Lady Who Swallowed a Fly" lyrics (available online; 1 copy per student)
- 1 copy of *The Follower*
- copies of Rhyme, Repetition, and Foreshadowing (page 84; 1 copy per student)
- Foreshadowing With Repetition Poetry Prompts (page 85), copied onto card stock and cut apart (1 card per student or per pair)

STEP BY STEP

1. Before reading *The Follower*, set the purpose for reading by reminding students that rhyme and repetition foreshadow events and create suspense. Explain that in this story, told in verse, the illustrations support the eerie foreshadowing by providing clues, which are not readily apparent.
2. Use a document camera to project the book, or hold it open, and read *The Follower* slowly, using a suspenseful, somewhat spooky tone of voice. Place emphasis on the bold, italicized words, which will lead students to see that the repetition is based upon the days of the week and builds consecutively as the week goes on.
3. As you complete each repetitive sequence, ask students if they know what "it" is yet. Have them raise their hands if they know the answer; however, do not have students share their responses until every hand in the class is raised. When everyone demonstrates an understanding that "it" is the cat, ask for a show of hands to indicate whether this discovery was based upon the text or the illustrations.

4. Invite students to complete the second part of the Rhyme, Repetition, and Foreshadowing graphic organizer with a partner. Afterward, ask partners to check their answers with a neighboring pair.

WRAP-UP

Explain to students that using repetition in writing and building upon previously repeated statements can create suspense and foreshadow an ending, regardless of whether the story is written in verse or as a novel.

Tell them that they are now going to have fun creating a short poem (6–8 lines) that includes foreshadowing and imitates the repetitive structure in *The Follower*. You may want to choose one prompt to model the activity for the class.

Pair students or allow students to work alone. Distribute one Poetry Prompt for Foreshadowing to each pair or to individual students. Encourage students to use their own ideas to create the poem if they prefer. Provide 10–15 minutes for students to write their foreshadowing poems. Build in a little extra time for sharing, if desired.

More Books for Teaching FORESHADOWING

Flotsam

Written and illustrated by David Wiesner
Clarion Books, 2006, 40 pp.

The very title of this amazing, wordless picture book foreshadows the treasures the reader will find between the pages. The definition of *flotsam* is something that floats on the water. And knowing this, we can instantly begin to make predictions about what the title foreshadows. A boy on vacation finds a camera that has been washed up on the shore. He develops the film inside it to discover photos of sea life too phantasmagorical to be real! Photos of the previous owners of the camera provide us with a window to past. Ultimately, another child takes ownership of the camera, and we are also gifted with a window to the future. Without words to constrain our imaginations, we are free to predict what will happen next, and every notion is possible.

TEACHING IDEA

■ As a whole class, create an outline for a story for *Flotsam*. Then divide students into groups or partners for writing text to accompany the pictures. Remind students to pay particular attention to what is foreshadowed and to address that in their stories.

INTERDISCIPLINARY CONNECTION

■ Using the zoom feature on a document camera, or a magnifying glass from a science lab, explore the photos in *Flotsam* to discover the very tiny surprises that David Wiesner has embedded in his artwork. Guide students to consider the beauty of the world too small for the naked eye and have them create descriptive poetry or prose to accompany photos they find in science books or similar online sites.

The Great Fuzz Frenzy

Written by Janet Stevens and Susan Stevens Crummel
Illustrated by Janet Stevens
Harcourt, 2005, 56 pp.

Who could imagine all the drama and chaos created when Violet the dog drops a florescent tennis ball down the tunnel of a prairie dog community? The prairie dogs are frightened at first and then puzzled by this object, but soon they are captivated by the fuzz of the ball and the many creative ways in which it can be manipulated. This story of adorable and cuddly creatures foreshadows the unexpected turns relationships can take when something new and covetous is added to an otherwise peaceful community. Before long, there is disharmony and argument in prairie-dog land that continues until one of them, Big Bark, takes all the fuzz away. Everything returns to its previous state only when the fuzz has been completely removed from the prairie-dog tunnels.

TEACHING IDEA

■ The green fuzz of a tennis ball seems at first glance to be a rather harmless thing. But its presence greatly impacts the prairie-dog community. Brainstorm a list of other items that might fall down into a prairie-dog tunnel, and ask students to develop alternative versions of the story, foreshadowing the impact of the brainstormed items on the prairie dogs. For instance, how would a jar of peanut butter or a roll of paper towels be received?

INTERDISCIPLINARY CONNECTION

■ The prairie-dog habitat is one of the most interesting living spaces of mammals. Invite students to find out more about the purpose of prairie-dog tunneling and compare it to other species that tunnel or create complex homes.

Henry's Freedom Box

Written by Ellen Levine
Illustrated by Kadir Nelson
Scholastic, 2007, 40 pp.

This book tells the true story of Henry Brown, a slave who escaped the South and mailed himself to freedom. The detailed and stunning artwork of Kadir Nelson helps the reader experience Henry's thoughts and feelings as he grows up enslaved, and overcomes one devastating experience after another. The artwork in this book plays a key role in foreshadowing the events to come as Henry grows up. After he is separated from his mother at a very young age, he goes to work in his master's tobacco factory. He begins to have as good a life as a slave can have, married to another slave and the father of three children. But soon more separation is foreshadowed in the story and as quickly as the turn of page, Henry's life is turned upside down as his family is sold away from him. Henry gathers his determination and plans to ship himself in a box to the North, where freedom lies. He is helped by abolitionists at both ends of his journey, ending up in Philadelphia as a free man.

TEACHING IDEA

■ Jot down the events in the story on index cards or slips of paper. Copy enough of the cards for the number of partner groups in the class. Ask partners to identify any clues that foreshadow the event on their card. After they have written the clue on the back of the card, call on partners to share their findings.

INTERDISCIPLINARY CONNECTION

■ Use this book as a stepping-off point for a unit on slavery and the Underground Railroad. Encourage students to research the amazing and various ways that slaves escaped and traveled north.

Meanwhile

Written and illustrated by Jules Feiffer
HarperCollins Publishers, 1997, 32 pp.

Meanwhile is the word in comic books that the writers use to change the scene, so when Raymond's mother calls him for some chore or another, Raymond "meanwhiles" his way through adventures as a pirate, a cowboy, and an astronaut. Who knew a word could be so powerful as to whisk him from one place to another, getting him out of danger in the nick of time? Each time he scribbles the word on a wall, the next adventure is foreshadowed, and the reader is left wondering how he will manage to get out of that predicament. The comic book style and the interaction between fantasy and reality are witty and ironic.

TEACHING IDEAS

■ Just as the word *meanwhile* can whisk the reader from scene to scene in a story, the word *furthermore* indicates that the writer will add more detail or additional information. "Furthermore" clues the reader in on something that is foreshadowed. Using a template for a comic book page, invite students to begin what may very well turn into a long-term project called "Furthermore."

■ Encourage students to use "However" to write several alternatives for one scene.

INTERDISCIPLINARY CONNECTIONS

■ Comic books, sometimes referred to now as graphic novels, cover topics as serious as history and science, and as lighthearted as romance and middle school. Lead the class on an exploration of the history of comics through virtual visits to the Museum of Comic and Cartoon Art, located in New York City.

■ Comic book versions are available for many of the classics and are sure to engage the reluctant reader.

Mrs. Marlowe's Mice

Written by Frank Asch
Illustrated by Devin Asch
Kids Can Press, 2007, 32 pp.

The reader's initial expectation for this lovely picture book may be a light story full of old-fashioned charm. But the endpapers foreshadow intrigue and espionage, and we are not disappointed when, on the first page, Mrs. Marlowe's "nervous swish of her tale" hints of danger. Mrs. Eleanor Marlowe is suspected by her neighbor to be harboring mice, and she is soon visited by the Department of Catland Security, whose uniforms evoke Gestapo-like comparisons. Mrs. Marlowe is quick on her cat feet to hide any traces of mouse presence in her home, and smooth of tongue in reassuring the authorities that she is not hiding any would-be fugitives. Fantastic illustrations and thoughtful character development contribute to the suspense involved in rescuing the mice from the claws of the enemy.

TEACHING IDEA

■ In this book, foreshadowing appears in the carefully written dialogue of the characters. Ask students to identify spoken lines on each page that give them a chill and signal their expectation of events to come. Use these lines and the high-level vocabulary in this book to write a "found poem" that builds suspense and engages the reader.

INTERDISCIPLINARY CONNECTION

■ The setting of *Mrs. Marlowe's Mice* and the vintage feel of the artwork evoke thoughts of Germany in the Second World War. In fact, there have been many times in history when the righteous acts of good people have saved innocent lives. Invite students to read more stories about everyday heroes and struggles for freedom in other picture books such as *Night Boat to Freedom, The Lily Cupboard, Henry's Freedom Box,* and *The Cats in Krasinski Square.*

Mr. Maxwell's Mouse

Written by Frank Asch
Illustrated by Devin Asch
Kids Can Press, 2004, 32 pp.

Mr. Maxwell is a well-to-do cat who has just achieved an enviable promotion in his firm. To make this day even more memorable, Mr. Maxwell orders a raw mouse for lunch, instead of his usual baked mouse. In the setting of a 1930s-era posh lunch club called the Paw and Claw, complete with cat musicians and elegant waiters, a cat-and-mouse tale is told in which the mouse outsmarts the accomplished and admired Mr. Maxwell. The ending, in which the mouse escapes his death by fork and knife, is foreshadowed throughout the story, when bit by bit the mouse distracts the cat with one ruse and then the next. Mr. Maxwell is distracted by the mouse's suggestions for salt first; then by his opinion of the wine list. A request for prayer is hilarious, and ultimately it is the mouse's ability to establish a personal relationship with Mr. Maxwell that aids in his freedom. It is impossible not to enjoy the building sense of this outcome, and be delighted by the trick, which results in escape for our mouse-hero and all his friends.

TEACHING IDEA

■ Ask students to identify the points in the story (*the mouse's distractions*) that foreshadow the conclusion and plot them on a story map, along with the climactic escape. Use the story map to illustrate rising, peaking, and falling action in the story. Discuss the way in which foreshadowing enhances the climax of the story. Reinforce this understanding by providing the opportunity for students to plot events and identify foreshadowing in self-selected picture books.

INTERDISCIPLINARY CONNECTION

■ For many students, a meal in an elegant restaurant

is an unfamiliar event. Help students develop prior knowledge by bringing in a variety of menus to peruse. While authentic menus are ideal, the Internet is also a great source for cuisine that is not available locally. Invite students to create a menu from a restaurant that serves their own favorite foods. Don't forget to require that they list appropriate pricing.

One Small Blue Bead

Written by Byrd Baylor
Illustrated by Ronald Himler
Maxwell Macmillan International, 1992, 32 pp.

In this story in verse, one small blue bead foreshadows the existence of other tribes about which the cave dwellers of our story know nothing. A wise old man is convinced that there must be other people who live similar lives beyond the mountains. The men in the tribe scoff at the idea, repeating over and over that there are no other people on earth. But the old man insists on searching, leaving a boy at home to take up his workload. From our vantage point of centuries in the future, we know that the old man will discover other people; yet we are thrilled by the return of the old man with proof in the form of a boy from another tribe, who wears the small blue bead.

TEACHING IDEA

Byrd Baylor uses an object, a small blue bead, to foreshadow the events of the story. The bead as a foreshadowing device brings us full circle from the present day, in which the bead is discovered, back into the past of the cave dwellers, and forward again to the present. Ask students to bring from home an object that can be used to inspire a story in which the object is a part of the lives of others in different time periods, as well as their own. Have students outline the story using a time line and tell it orally.

INTERDISCIPLINARY CONNECTION

The cave dwellers in the story express the same skepticism about the existence of other tribes as many people in our day and age have about life on other planets. Guide students to use logic and information available to them through research to prepare arguments for a debate about the existence of alien life forms. Encourage students to investigate both sides of the argument and stage a classroom debate with two opposing teams.

The Stranger

Written and illustrated by Chris Van Allsburg
Houghton Mifflin, 1986, 32 pp.

Exactly who is this stranger, whom Farmer Bailey accidentally runs into? Numerous hints foreshadow his identity. From the anachronistic clothing to a broken thermometer, the author gives us clue upon clue in both text and illustration, but no answers to who he might be. We can guess that the stranger has something to do with the changing of the season from summer to fall, but we get no confirmed answers from this eerie and peculiar tale. We can only guess from the stranger's parting message, "See you in the fall," that he is, indeed, some element of nature that brings the reds and yellows of autumn and vanquishes the greens of summer until next year. Perhaps the author intends that the real answers are what the readers come up with themselves.

TEACHING IDEA

Coming to a consensus about the main character of this book will be a challenge in any classroom. Using a word splash or a word web to brainstorm, ask students to identify all the foreshadowing and clues in the story that could contribute to a character sketch of the stranger. On a brown paper cutout of a human body, invite small groups of students to identify the stranger and describe exactly just who he is. Hang each group's completed paper characters, then compare the results.

INTERDISCIPLINARY CONNECTION

Celebrate the changing of the seasons at the beginning of the school year by creating nature collages composed of realia collected by students on a walk through the local woods, a park, or other nature area.

The Sweetest Fig

Written and illustrated by Chris Van Allsburg
Houghton Mifflin, 1993, 32 pp.

Monsieur Bibot is a dentist in Paris, who gets his just deserts in this magical tale of wishes coming true. A poor woman asks Bibot to help with a toothache, and then pays the greedy dentist with two figs, which she says have the power to make his dreams come true. His comeuppance is foreshadowed when, in his anger, he refuses to give the poor woman the pain pills for her tooth. Our disliking of this greedy man is deepened as we read about the way in which he mistreats his sweet little dog. The fig magic proves to be true when the dentist finds himself on the street in his underwear after eating the first fig. Bibot prepares to dream the perfect dream of wealth, when unbeknownst to him, Marcel the dog eats the fig instead. Foreshadowing is fulfilled on the final page of this ironic story as the good dog triumphs over the evil man.

TEACHING IDEA

■ Traditionally, folktales follow a common storyline in which magic is an uncontrollable element, and wishes made in earnest foreshadow a reversal of fortune, undercutting the main character's deepest hopes and desires. Direct students to identify the events of *The Sweetest Fig* on a graphic organizer such as a sequence chart, to indicate points of foreshadowing. Have a class discussion to compare these to events in traditional folktales to understand the formula for creating a story that keeps readers coming back for more.

INTERDISCIPLINARY CONNECTION

■ Chris Van Allsburg is known for his beautiful and often haunting illustrations done with sepia tones. Invite students to discover the uses of sepia in early photographs by searching the Internet for images and old postcards. Encourage students to try their hand at using brown and off-white in their own artistic renderings. Ask: *What mood are you able to create using only these two colors that might be more difficult to create using a full palette of color? Why?*

The Three Little Dassies

Written and illustrated by Jan Brett
G. P. Putnam's Sons, 2010, 32 pp.

In this delightful retelling of the story of *The Three Little Pigs*, dassies, or rock hyraxes, take on the role of the pigs. In this version, the dassies are the prey of an eagle rather than a wolf. They are dressed in the elaborate costume of Namibian women and are befriended by a lizard. Instead of huffing and puffing, the danger in this story is foreshadowed by the eagle's threats to "flap and clap" and blow their houses in. The repetition of the familiar lines forewarns the reader of what is to come, in the same manner with which we are familiar in the classic tale of the pigs. In this book, however, there is an added twist to the ending of the tale and we are left with a pourquoi story to boot. The eagle becomes charred by the fire from the dassies' stone home, and the story tells us that this is the reason that, to this day, eagles are black and dassies live in stone homes.

TEACHING IDEA

■ Careful examination of Jan Brett's signature artwork reveals clues to what is to come in the stories she illustrates. Have students work in writer/illustrator pairs to retell a familiar tale in a contemporary setting and make drawings that foreshadow events in subsequent pages.

INTERDISCIPLINARY CONNECTION

■ Create a book-flood of picture books, both fiction and nonfiction, that reflect the culture of Africa. Students can compare the various illustrations in the books to get a feeling for the wide variety of homes, clothing and life styles. Provide examples of African pourquoi tales and invite students to come up with their own creative reasons for occurrences in nature that would be worthy of a story. Use the brainstormed list for future writing opportunities.

Shortcut

Written and illustrated by Donald Crews
Mulberry Books, 1992, 32 pp.

Seven children, in a hurry to get home, decide to take a shortcut. They decide to walk on railroad tracks, rather than take the road home, and from the very beginning we know that this is not a good idea, and that something bad is foreshadowed. The narrator says and repeats, "We should have taken the road." We are told that the passenger trains have passed, but the freight trains have no schedule; another warning of danger. The cutoff to the road is passed, and more danger is foreshadowed. When the train whistle is heard at a distance, we feel the fear along with the characters in the story. Bold type in all capital letters screams, "GET OFF! GET OFF THE TRACKS!" And we are relieved when the "klakity klak" of the train passes by and all are safe. The children do not speak of this terrifying moment for a long time to come, and they never, *never* take the shortcut again.

TEACHING IDEA

■ Point out that repetition is a device used for foreshadowing that never fails to hook and reel in an audience. In particular, the phrase "We should have . . ." evokes a sense of apprehension. Have students decide upon one scenario and write a repeating line of foreshadowing that begins with "We should have . . . ." Provide an opportunity for peer-editing to help ensure that this single repeating line is captivating and foreshadows a good climax for the story the student will write.

INTERDISCIPLINARY CONNECTION

■ The history of train travel in this country is fascinating, and a plethora of both fiction and nonfiction books are available. Invite students to consider the importance of trains to the development of this country, and the ways in which it might have affected city life and rural communities differently.

FORESHADOWING IN FOUR VOICES

Name: ______________________________

At the end of each section of *Voices in the Park*, work with a partner to identify the examples of foreshadowing that appear in the text and the illustrations.

SECTION OF TEXT	EXAMPLE OF FORESHADOWING	EVENT FORESHADOWED
FIRST VOICE		
SECOND VOICE		
THIRD VOICE		
FOURTH VOICE		

RHYME, REPETITION, AND FORESHADOWING

Name: ____________________

After reading "The Old Lady Who Swallowed a Fly," answer with a partner each question about the rhyme on the chart below. Then, after listening to *The Follower*, answer these same questions about that tale.

TITLE OF LITERARY WORK	WHAT IS THE RHYME SCHEME AND STRUCTURE OF REPETITION?	HOW DOES THE REPETITIVE DEVICE BUILD ANTICIPATION OR SUSPENSE?	WHAT IS FORESHADOWED?	WHAT ARE DETAILS IN THE ILLUSTRATIONS THAT FORESHADOW?	HOW IS THE SURPRISE ENDING CREATED?
"THE OLD LADY WHO SWALLOWED A FLY"					
THE FOLLOWER					

POETRY PROMPTS FOR CREATING FORESHADOWING WITH REPETITION

ALL THOSE MONTHS I WAITED

In January, the snows came, and that meant . . .

(Use the months of the year and the corresponding weather as your structure.)

A VERY SPECIAL OUTFIT

I think that on my head I'll wear a hat and not just any hat. It will be a hat that . . .

(Use articles of clothing to describe a surprise outfit. Move down the body to describe each piece of apparel.)

A VALUABLE TEAMMATE

At the first game of the season, you would not have believed your eyes . . .

(Build your repetition and suspense by adding a new event to each game of the season.)

ARE WE THERE YET?

Our family piled into our station wagon and set out down the road. After 50 miles . . . After 100 miles . . .

(Structure your poem around stops on a road trip. Let your destination be a surprise!)

THE WEEK BEFORE MY BIRTHDAY

My birthday falls on next Thursday, and I have so long to wait . . .

(Use the days of the week to foreshadow how you will spend your birthday next week.)

ROCKETS ARE NOT THE ONLY THINGS WITH COUNTDOWNS!

I'm counting down to _______ , and then I will _______ . Ten! It will take ten hours to _______ . Nine! It will take reading nine books before I can . . .

(Use the countdown to foreshadow what kind of blast off you are expecting.)

I'VE LOOKED EVERYWHERE

I have looked in my pockets and could not find _______ . I have looked in my room and seen neither hide nor hair of _______ . Next I checked the kitchen, and could not find it.

(Create foreshadowing during your search by building to finding something that will surprise the reader.)

HOLIDAY HAPPENINGS

I was pretty sure my favorite holiday was New Year's Day and that's because on New Year's Day, we _______ . But on second thought, my favorite holiday could be President's Day because on President's Day we _______ .

(Use holidays in chronological order to foreshadow. Describe the way you celebrate, including the previous holiday description as you progress.)

CHAPTER 7 • FLASHBACK

"My heels click faster and faster on the sidewalk. That sound pulls me back to that time not so many years ago. I drift back. And back some more. . ."

—from *Langston's Train Ride* (page 6)

A flashback is a literary device in which an earlier episode, conversation, or event is inserted into the sequence of events. Many times, flashbacks are presented as a memory of the narrator or of another character.

In the example above, the author uses verbal clues to craft a flashback in which Langston Hughes flashes back to the year 1920, when he was 18 years old. Writers use flashback to make a comparison between the present action and something that happened in the past, or to provide additional background information about the characters. As readers explore flashback in stories, they can consider how the flashback adds tension to the narrative and what they learn from the character's past. In addition to using literature to introduce examples of flashback, provide explicit examples by showing appropriate clips from films, such as *Titanic* or *Holes*.

By exploring and discussing flashback in both literature and film, you can focus on students' comprehension, interpretation, and evaluation of the device and its application in their own writing.

LESSON 13

Flashing Back in Time

MODEL TEXT

In My Own Backyard
Written by Judi Kurjian
Illustrated by David Wagner
Charlesbridge, 1993, 32 pp.

A young child looks out the window of her backyard and wonders what it may have looked like in the past. With beautiful illustrations and brief descriptive sentences, the book takes a brief look at the evolution of life on Earth. This exploration into the past is clearly marked by changes in the illustrations and short paragraphs.

CRITICAL QUESTION

How does the author use flashback to depict the history of life on Earth?

MATERIALS

- 1 copy of *In My Own Backyard*
- plain white paper
- markers, colored pencils
- copies of Time Line Flashback (page 93; 1 copy per student)
- chart paper
- computers
- art supplies

WARM-UP

Distribute sheets of plain white paper to students. Ask them to hold the paper horizontally and to fold it in half. Instruct students to title the left side "present" and the right side "past."

Next, direct students to imagine that they are looking out their bedroom window into their backyard or the back of their dwelling place. Tell them to draw on the left side of their paper a quick sketch of what they see. Provide a few minutes for students to complete their drawings.

Then, ask students to transport themselves back in time 100 years. Invite them to imagine what their backyard looked like 100 years ago. Instruct them to sketch their "flashback" on the right side of their paper.

Afterward, pair students and have them share their drawings. Encourage them to compare the two illustrations and to discuss the differences they observe.

STEP BY STEP

1. Explain to students that, like the author of *In My Own Backyard*, they used the view from their bedroom window to create a flashback portrait of their backyard as it might have looked 100 years ago. Emphasize that the author uses this same technique to take the reader on a geological journey through time.
2. Distribute the Time Line Flashback reproducible to students. Inform them that as you read *In My Own Backyard* aloud, you will stop at various points and ask them to use some words and some pictures to show the reverse chronology of the flashback.
3. Place a piece of chart paper at the front of the room. Then, using a document camera, project a copy of the text onto a screen, or hold the book open. Instruct students to listen for verbal clues and to look for visual clues that show that the author is moving out of the present into the past. Begin reading the text aloud.
4. Stop at the bottom of page 4. Ask students what the narrator is doing as he or she looks out the window. Guide students to see that the narrator is daydreaming, which is a common flashback technique.
5. Read to the bottom of page 12. Ask students how the author signaled the transition from the present to the past and from one flashback to the next. Record their responses on the chart paper. Afterward, provide a few minutes for students to draw pictures and record words in the first segment of their Time Line Flashback to show the time period covered so far in the story.
6. Continue the process of reading, stopping, and recording verbal clues that connote time transitions, and provide time for students to work on their Time Line Flashback. Stopping points include the bottom of pages 16, 18, 22, 26, and 28.
7. At the end of the book, ask students what technique the author uses to bring the reader back into the present.
8. After students complete the Time Line Flashback, show students the book's time line and have them compare and contrast their time line to the book's.

WRAP-UP

Invite students to write and illustrate their own version of *In My Own Backyard*. If students have access to technology, ask them to look through their bedroom window and take a photograph of their backyard.

To create their journey back through time, students can upload photos and images from the Internet and use photo presentation software to design a narrated slide show. The narration for each photo should incorporate verbal clues that transition the viewer from the present into the past and back again. Before beginning the project, remind students of copyright laws and demonstrate how they should cite their sources. Students who do not have access to technology can make flashback scrapbooks instead.

LESSON 14

Flashing Back With Dreams

MODEL TEXT

Beardream
Written by Will Hobbs
Illustrated by Jill Kastner
Atheneum Books for Young Readers, 1997, 32 pp.

Short Tail, a Ute boy, becomes very concerned when the Great Bear fails to come out of hibernation during the first signs of spring. Fearing that the bear will become sick, Short Tail decides to climb the mountains. During his arduous journey, Short Tail becomes very tired and falls asleep and dreams. In the dream, Short Tail finds the Great Bear and explains to it that everyone is very concerned for its safety and well-being. The Great Bear, aware of the mutual respect demonstrated by Short Tail, decides to help him and invites him to take part in a secret. He takes Short Tail to a magical place where all the bears perform a celebration dance to commemorate the beginning of a new season. He is told to share this dance with his people; then he wakes up from the dream. When he awakes he returns to his people and tells them about his dream. From then on, the people perform this dance to celebrate the end of winter and the awakening of the bears. This story is based upon a version of the story common among the Utes of Colorado and Utah.

CRITICAL QUESTION

How does the author use the dream flashback technique to convey the theme of the story?

NOTE: As stated by Will Hobbs, the theme of this book is that humankind is an integral part of nature.

WARM-UP

Share with your students a personal anecdote about connecting with an animal. For many people the bond with a pet is so deep that they will attribute human thoughts and tendencies to the animal. It is natural that our pets will find their way into our dreams as a way of completing the communication.

MATERIALS

- 1 copy of *Beardream*
- copies of Animal Dreams (page 94; 1 copy per student)
- chart paper
- copies of Tracking Dream Flashbacks (page 95; 1 copy per student)
- scissors
- markers, colored pencils
- construction paper
- glue sticks

Ask students to portray a dream or a deep connection that they may have had with a pet or an animal by brainstorming on the Animal Dreams graphic organizer. They may use words or drawings.

In groups, ask students to share what they have brainstormed, identifying similarities in their animal relationships. Ask them to separate the features of their relationship that might be generalized to humankind's relationship with animals and to specify which features demonstrate their own unique relationships with their pet.

Debrief as a class, concluding with a list of features that identify qualities in humankind's relationship with animals. Post this list on chart paper to refer to during discussion of *Beardream*.

STEP BY STEP

1. Before reading *Beardream* aloud to the class, explain that the chronological sequence of this story is interrupted by a bear's dream flashback and the flashback of a boy called Short Tail. Stress that in the story it is often difficult to distinguish the real world from the dream world and the bear's dream from the boy's dream. Ask students to listen to the story the first time to identify the moments in which a dream world is entered and by whom.
2. Using a document camera, or by holding up the book, display and read *Beardream*.
3. Distribute to students copies Tracking Dream Flashbacks and scissors. Ask students to cut out the footprints.

4. Read through the story again, this time instructing students to identify text clues that indicate the bear's dream and the boy's dream. They should write the text clues appropriately on either a paw print or a footprint.
5. Pair up students so they can compare their footprints and paw prints. Pass out large construction paper and glue sticks and have partners create chronological footpath sequence charts. Post charts and invite student pairs to share their thoughts with the class.

WRAP-UP

Ask students to think of a novel they have read that included a human's relationship with an animal. Invite them to call out titles and write them on the board. Most students will have read a trade book that will work for this activity. Some examples of titles would be *Old Yeller, Where the Red Fern Grows, Thomasina, Emmy and the Incredible Shrinking Rat, The Black Stallion,* and *My Side of the Mountain.*

Instruct students to select from the list of books on the board one of the animals with which they are familiar and to write a dream-story for that animal that could be inserted into the book. Mention that doing this activity requires using personification—a figure of speech that gives the qualities of a person to an animal, an object, or an idea.

More Books for Teaching FLASHBACK

Aunt Mary's Rose

Written by Douglas Wood
Illustrated by LeUyen Pham
Candlewick Press, 2010, 32 pp.

This beautifully illustrated picture book takes readers on a nostalgic trip through one family's history. Aunt Mary explains that the rosebush in her backyard has been in the family since before she was born. Young Douglas is learning to take care of this precious plant and, in doing so, learns more about his family. This selection celebrates the connection between families and love from generation to generation.

TEACHING IDEA

During reading, ask students to jot down the specific events and emotions that the author used to describe the flashback. After reading, ask students to discuss how the flashback in the story helped them understand what happened in the story.

INTERDISCIPLINARY CONNECTION

Invite students to conduct an oral history project using Web 2.0 technologies to capture details about the lives of their grandparents or about individuals in a nearby retirement community.

Bird

Written by Zetta Elliott
Illustrated by Shadra Strickland
Lee & Low, 2008, 48 pp.

This Storytelling World Honor Award–winning selection for adolescents introduces readers to Bird, an African-American boy who loves to draw. He uses drawing as an escape from the despondency that sometimes surrounds his life. In particular, he likes to draw birds. Throughout the story, Bird enjoys listening to his grandfather's stories about being a wartime pilot. However, his big brother, Marcus, has started taking drugs and his apparent physical and emotional decline lead him to his early death. Bird pays tribute to his brother and the good memories that he has by drawing him into his artwork.

TEACHING IDEA

Since the artwork in this book helps convey various emotions, bring in other pieces for conversation. Invite students to examine the artwork or images from reputable museum and gallery websites. Ask students to consider how the work elicits memories or emotions from their lives and have them write their thoughts in a journal.

INTERDISCIPLINARY CONNECTION

Birds are a recurring theme in this selection. Ask students to research more about why the author decided to use birds as the motif in this story.

The Cemetery Keepers of Gettysburg

Written by Linda Oatman High
Illustrated by Laura Francesca Filippucci
Walker & Company, 2007, 32 pp.

This beautifully illustrated book pays tribute to the Thorn family, who were the cemetery keepers at Gettysburg's Evergreen Cemetery. The story is narrated by Ted, who explains how his family was affected by war. He shares the story of his father, who left to fight for the Union, and that his pregnant mother, two brothers, and grandparents were left behind to tend to the cemetery. Before the battle reached them, they escaped, only to return to death and destruction. The family spent many days digging graves for more than one hundred soldiers from both sides and, in this way, were able to honor those who had lost their lives.

TEACHING IDEA

- With partners, have students determine how the author provides insight into the narrator's character and how the flashback contributes to the mood of the story.

INTERDISCIPLINARY CONNECTIONS

- This selection is ideal to use during a unit about the Civil War.
- Use this book to reinforce the literary element of theme.
- Ask students to think about famous people (from today or from history) whom they admire and the characteristics that these individuals demonstrate. Invite students to research and report on those whom students feel exemplify admirable qualities.

Kamishibai Man

Written and illustrated by Allen Say
Houghton Mifflin, 2005, 32 pp.

In Japanese, *kamishibai* means "paper theatre," and during Allen Say's childhood, he remembers the kamishibai man who used to sell sweets and tell tales of heroes and heroines, using picture cards and a wooden stage. In this nostalgic story, Grandpa, once a kamishibai man, wants to share his show with local children. He finds a vacant lot and returns to his childhood memories, and finds himself surrounded by a crowd of adults who remember him from their childhood.

TEACHING IDEA

- After reading, ask students to record their text-to-text and text-to-self connections to the selection. Invite students to describe how the use of flashback helped them understand the story.

INTERDISCIPLINARY CONNECTION

- This selection is ideal to use in a text set about Japanese culture. Arrange for the class to work with the art teacher to create group kamishibai storytelling cards. You may find examples at www.kamishibai.com.

Langston's Train Ride

Written by Robert Burleigh
Illustrated by Leonard Jenkins
Orchard, 2004, 32 pp.

In this historical-fiction picture book, the reader is transported through the memories of Langston Hughes back in time to the day when he began to accomplish his dream of becoming a writer. Using flashback, the author tells about the moment when Langston Hughes wrote his famous poem "The Negro Speaks of Rivers," while on a train ride to Mexico to visit his father. Burleigh's words move with the rhythm of the train's rocking motion, and we join Langston as he drifts off to the sounds of the train's clackity clack. The observant reader becomes aware of a flashback within this memory as Langston thinks about all of the history that the rivers and his people have shared. The landscape that blurs as Langston stares out the train window is the backdrop for his thoughts about slavery and the Mississippi River; and Africa and the Nile. The poem is born on a piece of an old envelope, and we are flashed forward to the present as crowds clamber to hear Langston read his words.

TEACHING IDEA

Ask students to think back on a time in their lives when they accomplished something important to them, and write about that moment as if they were reliving the event. Invite students to share their original flashbacks.

INTERDISCIPLINARY CONNECTION

Train travel in this country has diminished substantially, and has all but vanished as a means of vacation transportation. Commuter trains carry passengers in and out of cities, but long train trips are the exception rather than the rule. Ask small groups of students to use the Internet to investigate and plan a long train trip. Require them to determine the length of the trip, the cost of the ticket, and the route of travel. Extend the activity by asking them to create a travel brochure.

Music for Alice

Written and illustrated by Allen Say
Houghton Mifflin, 2004, 32 pp.

This book is based on the true story of Alice Sumida, whose passion for dancing was put aside during the imminent challenges of being Japanese-American during World War II. With immaculate storytelling and watercolor paintings, the author shares Alice's memories, including her passion for dancing. This story pays tribute to the life of a woman whose perseverance and resilience will inspire readers to see that dreams can be fulfilled, even when least expected.

TEACHING IDEA

Play a selection of classical music and ask students to close their eyes and visualize a memory or image. Then invite them to write about this visualization. After freewriting, ask students to consider how *Music for Alice* uses flashback.

INTERDISCIPLINARY CONNECTION

This is an excellent historical-fiction picture book to integrate into a unit about the challenges endured by many Japanese Americans during World War II.

My Mama Had a Dancing Heart

Written by Libba Moore Gray
Illustrated by Raúl Colón
Orchard Books, 1995, 32 pp.

In this story, a young woman looks back upon her mother's joyous take on life and pays tribute to the many childhood memories shared by mother and daughter. The gentle moods and emotions around a mother-daughter relationship are told through lyrical language.

TEACHING IDEA

The flashback in this story occurs when the character transitions back to her childhood memories. Ask students to think about something that is going on in their lives right now and then invite them to write a short explanation of why they think this situation occurred.

INTERDISCIPLINARY CONNECTION

Ask students to compose their own memoirs using photographs and images from one childhood memory.

Pemba Sherpa

Written by Olga Cossi
Illustrated by Gary Bernard
Odyssey Books, 2009, 32 pp.

Featured on the 2011 Amelia Bloomer Project list, this book shares the story of a courageous young girl named Yang Ki. She is from Nepal and dreams of becoming a Sherpa guide, despite the preconceived notions of women's roles in her community. She enlists the help of her older brother to build up the skills necessary to become a guide; however, he laughs at her foolishness. Her persistence and courage are demonstrated throughout the book, and she secretly follows her brother up the trail and comes to his rescue in a time of need.

TEACHING IDEA

Ask students to consider what memories the writer shares to tell this story and whether the story elicits any of their own memories.

INTERDISCIPLINARY CONNECTION

■ Not only is this selection ideal to integrate during Women's History month, but it is also excellent for sparking writing about personal courage.

Pink and Say

Written and illustrated by Patricia Polacco
Philomel Books, 1994, 48 pp.

In this historical-fiction picture book, Pink, a young black soldier rescues Say, a wounded white soldier from the battlefield. Pink brings Say home, where his mother, Moe Moe Bay, nurses him back to health. Moe Moe is killed by marauders, and the two young men are captured and taken to Andersonville prison. Pink is hanged there a few hours after arrival. Polacco's great-great-grandfather Say spent his life sharing this story because he felt guilty for living when "a more worthy human had died," leaving behind neither birth certificate, death certificate, grave, nor family to remember him.

TEACHING IDEA

■ Throughout this story, the author employs many literary elements, including flashback. Ask students to work with a partner to plot the specific events that describe the flashback.

INTERDISCIPLINARY CONNECTIONS

■ Ask students to research family stories to share with the class for an oral history project.

■ Invite students to write about simple acts of kindness that they have performed and then share their stories with a partner.

So Far From the Sea

Written by Eve Bunting
Illustrated by Chris K. Soentpiet
Clarion Books, 1998, 32 pp.

A young Japanese-American girl tells how she and her family visit the site at Manzanar, where her father was interned as a child in 1942 and where her grandfather died, heartbroken.

TEACHING IDEA

■ The illustrations help explain the struggles of life at the internment camp. Using the illustrations as a springboard, ask students to share the emotions that are evoked on each page. Ask students to consider how the flashback and use of illustrations helped them understand the story.

INTERDISCIPLINARY CONNECTION

■ This story is ideal to use in a text set to conduct additional research about the lives of Japanese-American families during World War II.

The Sunsets of Miss Olivia Wiggins

Written by Lester L. Laminack
Illustrated by Constance R. Bergum
Peachtree, 1998, 32 pp.

When her daughter, Angel, and her great-grandson Troy come to visit her in a nursing home, Miss Olivia Wiggins doesn't appear to notice their presence. Small things that they both say and do bring back memories for her. For example, when Troy hums a tune by her chair, Miss Olivia remembers holding her babies and singing to them. The smell of lilacs helps her remember a spring day with her husband. This tender story reminds us to value and maintain our relationships, even when they are altered by Alzheimer's disease.

TEACHING IDEA

■ Ask students to think about how Troy's actions help Miss Olivia rekindle memories of her past.

INTERDISCIPLINARY CONNECTIONS

■ Ask students to think about a person who matters to them. Invite them to list all the small moments that they remember with this person. Students can use this information to write a poem or letter to that person.

■ Encourage students to select a family photo and write a descriptive piece based on that photo.

TIME LINE FLASHBACK

Name: ______________________________

Write words above the time line and draw pictures below it to show the reverse chronology of the flashback in the book *In My Backyard*. After completing your time line, compare and contrast it with the one in the book.

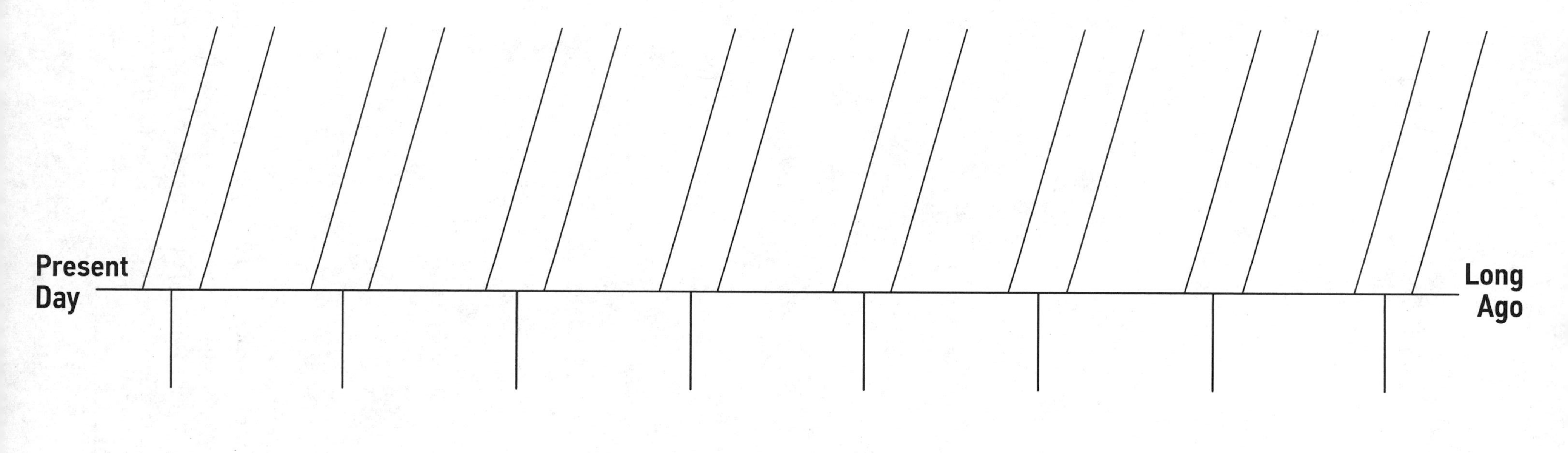

ANIMAL DREAMS

Name: ______________________________

Using colored pencils or markers, brainstorm with words and images moments and feelings you have dreamed of or experienced with a favorite pet, or possibly an animal you have observed in the wild. If you do not have a pet, imagine the relationship you would like to have with an animal. You may use the different paw segments to separate feelings or moments.

TRACKING DREAM FLASHBACKS

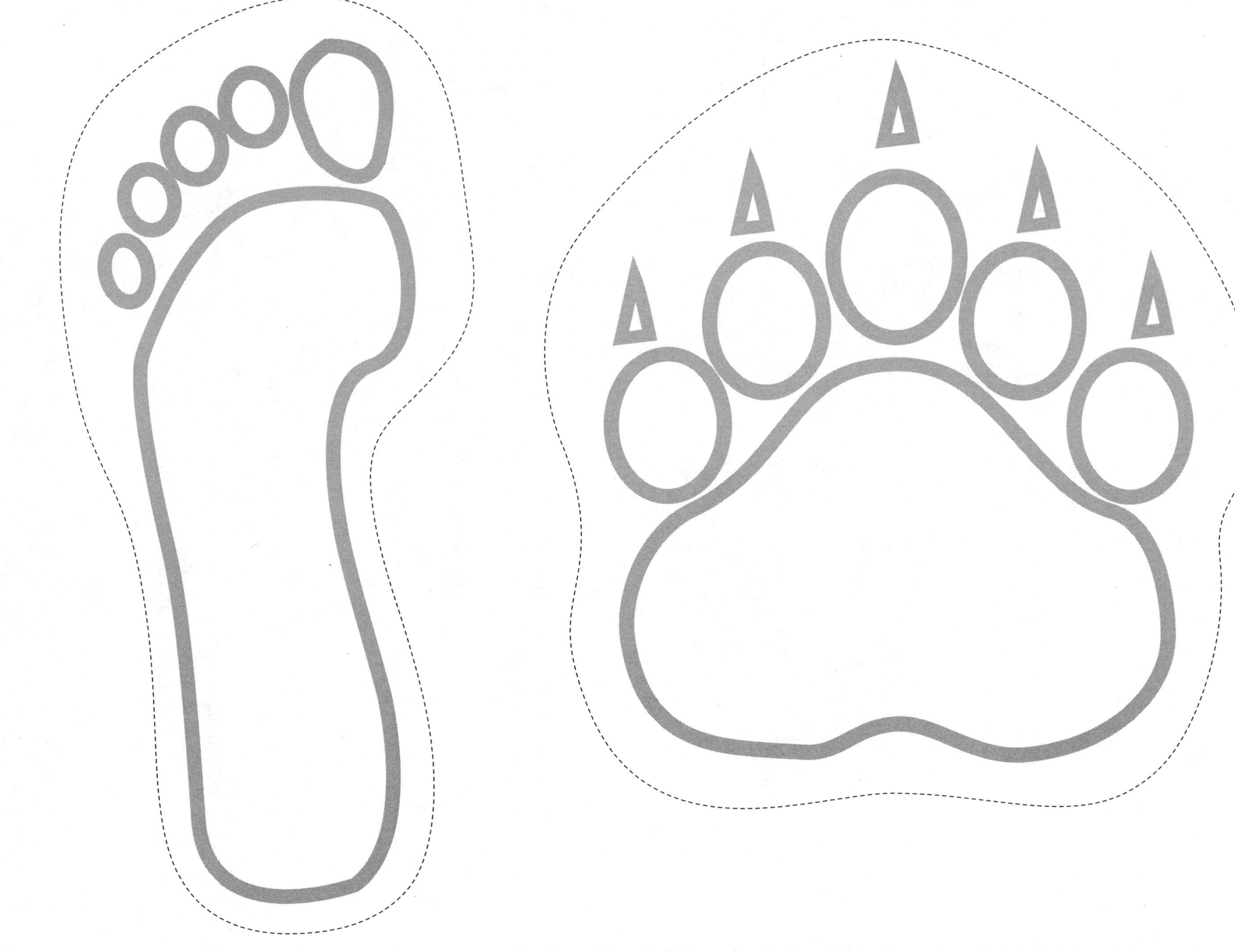

CHAPTER 8 • FIGURATIVE LANGUAGE

"My abuelita is round. Robust, she says, like a* calabaza*. A pumpkin."

—from *My Abuelita* (page 9)

Whenever authors describe something by comparing it with something else, they are employing figurative language. This refers to any language that goes beyond the literal meaning of words in order to furnish new or fresh insights into an idea or a subject. Some of the most common types of figurative language include simile, metaphor, personification, and hyperbole.

SIMILE: A figure of speech that involves a direct comparison between two unlike things, usually with the words *like* or *as*.

METAPHOR: A figure of speech that implies a comparison between two relatively unlike things.

PERSONIFICATION: A figure of speech that gives the qualities of a person to an animal, an object, or an idea.

HYPERBOLE: An exaggerated statement used to heighten effect and to emphasize a point.

By developing an understanding of figurative language, students can comprehend literary works more deeply and use figurative language in their own work. You can facilitate this through read-alouds, modeling, and student-centered engagements.

LESSON 15

Similes

MODEL TEXT

My Abuelita

Written by Tony Johnston
Illustrated by Yuyi Morales and photographed by Tim O'Meara
Harcourt Children's Books 2009, 32 pp.

In this book, a recipient of the Pura Belpré Honor Book Award for illustration, a young boy who lives with his grandmother describes how she gets ready for work every day, along with him and her cat, Frida Kahlo. The little boy has to remind her to get dressed and to take what she needs for work, such as stalks of maize. The beautiful illustrations evoke a happy and affectionate feeling. The meaning of the Spanish words is clear within the context of the story.

MATERIALS

- 1 copy of *My Abuelita*
- plain white paper
- chart paper
- markers, colored pencils
- 1 copy of the Simile Portrait Model (page 104; transparency or scanned to project onto a screen)
- copies of a Simile Portrait (page 105; 1 copy per student)

CRITICAL QUESTION

How do similes enhance character descriptions?

WARM-UP

To introduce simile, write several examples on the board. Consider using the following examples:

- The snow fell from the sky like a parade of tiny, silky parachutes.
- In the sunlight, the lines on Grandpa's forehead looked as deep as the Grand Canyon.
- The wind whistled like a train speeding toward its destination.
- Grandma's hugs were as warm as a downy quilt on a blustery day.

First, define the term *simile*—a comparison of two dissimilar objects that uses *like* or *as*. Next, acquaint students with the following guidelines for how to interpret similes:

- Identify the simile.
- Decide which two things are being compared.
- Discuss the similarities between the two things.
- Visualize or draw what the simile makes you see.

As a class, practice applying the strategy for interpreting similes. For example, when examining the first simile above, "like a parade of tiny, silky parachutes," have students identify the simile. Next, ask them what two objects are being compared (*snowflakes and tiny parachutes*). Then direct students to explain the similarities between snowflakes and tiny parachutes (*both are light and float down to earth; both fill the sky*). Finally, ask students to describe what the simile makes them visualize. Interpret the second simile as a class and then have partners work together to interpret the remaining similes.

STEP BY STEP

1. Before reading *My Abuelita* aloud, explain to students that the narrator uses highly original similes to describe his grandmother. State that many of the similes provide the reader with rich details about both the grandmother's appearance and her personality.
2. Distribute paper to students and tell them to record similes that describe the grandmother or "abuelita" as they listen to the story.
3. Using a document camera, project the text onto a screen, or hold the book open. Begin reading aloud and stop at the bottom of page 5. Ask students to identify the similes on that page. Discuss what the similes reveal about the grandmother. Continue reading to the end of the story.
4. After reading, have students share the similes they recorded and write them down on a piece of chart paper. If the list is incomplete, go back to the story and add to it. Here are some examples of similes in the book:

   PAGE 5: "She is as old as the hills, she says. Maybe older."

   PAGE 5: "Her face is as crinkled as a dried *chile*."

   PAGE 6: "She does knee bends and breathes deep, oh deep. Like a big salty whale out at sea."

   PAGE 9: "My abuelita is round. Robust, she says, like a *calabaza*. A pumpkin."

   PAGE 10: "'Isn't it thrilling to sing like a frog?' she asks me."

   PAGE 12: "She looks like a great big bee. While she dries, she hums like a great big bee getting ready for work."

   PAGE 19: "She always says the words should be as round as dimes and as wild as blossoms blooming."

   PAGE 20: "'¡Ay! I feel like a wild blossom blooming,' my abuelita says."

   PAGE 20: "She puts on a flowery gown and bright red shoes and a scarf like a cloud that flows down to the ground."
5. Assign small groups of students a simile from the list to interpret and draw. To assist students with this process, refer back to the guidelines for interpreting similes. Encourage each student within a group to draw the assigned simile; this will help illustrate that readers can interpret similes in different ways. Remind students to discuss what the simile teaches them about the grandmother.

6. Have one member from each group share the group's interpretation and visualization of the simile assigned.
7. As a whole class, discuss how the similes impact the reader's perceptions of the character. What do the similes reveal about Abuelita's character? How would the reader's perspective of Abuelita change if the similes were removed from the story? For example, how does the statement "Her face is as crinkled as a dried *chile*" (page 5) differ from one such as "My Abuelita has wrinkles on her face"?

WRAP-UP

Have students brainstorm a list of older people about whom they care deeply and then choose one as the subject of their simile portrait.

Explain to students that, like the narrator in *My Abuelita*, they are going to create a poem that uses similes to describe a loved one. Project onto a screen the Simile Portrait Model and tell students that this model is based on the reproducible scaffold you will provide to them. Then read the poem aloud.

Distribute a Simile Portrait writing frame to students and have them use it to write the rough draft of their poem. Keep the model poem on the screen so that students can refer to it as they draft.

Direct students to creatively write, type, and illustrate their poems. Encourage them to include on their final copy a photo of the person they portrayed. Then create a classroom portrait gallery and have students invite friends and family members for a gallery tour.

LESSON 16

Hyperbole

MODEL TEXT

Dust Devil

Written by Anne Isaacs

Illustrated by Paul O. Zelinsky

Schwartz & Wade Books, 2010, 48 pp.

Angelica Longrider, aka Swamp Angel, captures our hearts and smiles in this wild and frolicking tall tale set in the wilds of Montana. In need of a horse that can accommodate her great size, Angel wrangles and tames a dust storm. Inside of it she finds a perfectly sized horse, whom she names Dust Devil. Their wild and crazy adventures take them head to head with the bandit Backward Bart and throughout the Old West, where our heroine's actions are instrumental in forming and explaining natural phenomena along the way.

CRITICAL QUESTION

How does hyperbole emphasize a point or create a humorous effect?

MATERIALS

- 1 copy of *Dust Devil*
- plain white paper
- sticky notes
- chart paper
- index cards (1 card per student)
- copies of Hyperbole and Caricatures (1 copy per student; page 106)
- copies of A Hyperbole Portrait (1 copy per student; page 107)

WARM-UP

Activate students' background knowledge of the hyperbole used in tall tales and folk tales by writing the following phrase on the board:

He was so big that __________.

Challenge pairs of students to discuss how to make this person really seem bigger than life. As a whole class, share ideas of how to complete the sentence.

Then have partners complete the following statements on a sheet of paper:

She was so small that __________.

The student was so loud that __________.

Invite pairs to share their ideas with another pair. Then ask these new groups of four to choose one statement to share with the entire class and to write it on a sticky note. Appoint one group member to share the statement with the rest of the class. Have this individual post the group's sticky note on a piece of chart paper so the class can refer to it when they write their hyperboles.

As a class, discuss what the statements have in common. Steer students toward the idea of exaggeration. Explain that they have created statements called hyperboles and then share the definition: hyperbole is a deliberate exaggeration used to emphasize a point or to create an effect.

STEP BY STEP

1. Emphasize that hyperbole is the foundation of tall tales and is often used in humorous writing as well.
2. Distribute an index card to each student. Write the word *hyperbole* on the board and have students write it in large letters on their index cards. Tell them to listen for examples of hyperbole during the upcoming read-aloud and to show you their index card when they hear one.
3. Using a document camera, project a copy of the text onto a screen, or hold the book open for all to see. Read aloud *Dust Devil.*
4. After reading, ask students to share some of the memorable hyperboles from the book and ask them to describe the effect of the hyperbole on the story.
5. Distribute to students copies of Hyperbole and Caricatures. Direct students to record hyperboles related to Backward Bart's size and actions, as you reread pages 18–23. Stop at the bottom of each page to provide time for students to write. Emphasize that Bart is a Desperado, so actions attributed to the gang are also things Bart does.
6. After students collect the hyperboles, pair them and ask them to analyze the effects the hyperboles have on the reader's understanding of Bart's character. Then discuss their responses as a whole class.

WRAP-UP

Distribute copies of A Hyperbole Portrait. Invite students to super-size their physical features as they draw a caricature of themselves. Then direct students to create three original hyperboles that exaggerate admirable qualities and traits friends and family members attribute to them. Instruct students to write these hyperboles beneath their caricature. Display the caricatures around the room and have students guess which classmate is being portrayed.

More Books for Teaching FIGURATIVE LANGUAGE

Elena's Serenade

Written by Campbell Geeslin
Illustrated by Ana Juan
Atheneum Books for Young Readers, 2004, 40 pp.

In this magical tale created with a Mexican backdrop, Elena must set off on a journey of the heart to learn glassblowing. Her father has told her that girls can't blow glass, so, disguised in her brother's clothing, she determines to prove him wrong. Elena's glassblowing pipette ends up making music as well as beautiful glass. Her father welcomes her home and she realizes her dream of working with him side by side. This book's pages are overflowing with simile, metaphors, and onomatopoeia.

TEACHING IDEA

■ Have students compare the character of Elena with other famous literary or fairy tale characters who had to don a disguise to accomplish their goal. Instruct them to write a skit and act out a dialogue between Elena and the character with whom she is being compared.

INTERDISCIPLINARY CONNECTION

■ Invite students to research the art of glassblowing and consider the skills needed to be successful at this craft.

The Hickory Chair

Written by Lisa Rowe Fraustino
Illustrated by Benny Andrews
Arthur Levine Books, 2001, 32 pp.

In this realistic and warm story about the relationship between a grandmother and Louis, her "favorite youngest" grandson, the author uses the rich imagery of sound, smell, and touch to describe Louis's life as a child born blind into a loving family. When his grandmother dies, it is Louis who is able to discover all the notes that are clues to Grandmother's legacy; all except for the note that tells what grandmother has left for him. Ultimately Louis's "blind sight" leads him to the message that confirms that his grandmother's favorite chair was indeed meant for him.

TEACHING IDEA

■ Place interesting objects in brown paper lunch bags. Invite students to touch, smell, or taste the objects. Once they have been returned to the bags (with the exception of any items "tasted"), give students time to respond by creating diamante or cinquain poems rich in the descriptive language of the senses.

INTERDISCIPLINARY CONNECTION

■ Encourage students to investigate famous people in history who have accomplished amazing things despite (or because of) disabilities. Students can follow up by writing an acceptance speech for an award from the perspective of the famous person.

In November

Written by Cynthia Rylant
Illustrated by Jill Kastner
Harcourt Brace, 2000, 32 pp.

During November, the world is tucking itself into its winter bed. This in-between season is described in rich, poetic language and illustrated with vivid oil paintings. The sensory language of colors, similes, and metaphors evokes the feelings and smells of harvest and Thanksgiving. Rylant's verbal images are simply painted, with warm autumn colors and a sleepiness that foreshadows hibernation. The feeling of warmth from being huddled together to ward off the cold is experienced alike by insects, barn animals, and humans.

TEACHING IDEA

■ Using the color palette of *In November*, invite students to write color poems describing their favorite things about this month of the year. Have students use a color poem template (such as the ones on pages 71 and 72). They should write their poem in marker on construction paper, and decorate the background with colored tissue paper to create a collage. Create a bulletin board of student work.

INTERDISCIPLINARY CONNECTION

■ Have students work in groups to research animals that flourish and thrive in different seasons and climates, and compare them to the North American animals illustrated in the book *In November*. Groups should make a poster comparing the details about the lives of two of the animals they investigated.

Ladder to the Moon

Written by Maya Soetoro-Ng
Illustrated by Yuyi Morales
Candlewick Press, 2011, 48 pp.

In this tale, we join Suhaila as she dreams about getting to know her deceased grandmother. Suhaila's mother describes Grandma as being like the moon, and so the moon becomes Suhaila's dream destination for discovery. From this vantage point, she hears stories of people all over the world in their struggle to survive through disasters of weather, war, and other turmoil. Sensory language and detailed description allow us to share as Suhaila's knowledge of the world and empathy for humanity grows.

TEACHING IDEA

- Invite students to choose something in nature (such as a tree or the sun) as a metaphor for a beloved family member, friend, or grandparent. Students should draw a large outline of their chosen metaphor and then do a word-splash on the drawing, using descriptive language that connects their selected person with that object.

INTERDISCIPLINARY CONNECTION

- Ask students to investigate and consider the world's response to recent disasters we have experienced such as Hurricane Katrina, or the 2011 earthquake and tsunami in Japan. Students should make a graph or chart that shows the amount of assistance and aid sent by volunteer organizations. Then, in small groups, they can discuss the importance of volunteerism and brainstorm ideas for student volunteering at a local level.

Odetta: The Queen of Folk

Written and illustrated by Stephen Alcorn
Scholastic Press, 2010, 40 pp.

This book tells the story of spiritual and folk music legend Odetta. With humor entrenched in biographical detail, we read about her growing up in "Burning Ham," Alabama, within the confines of the Jim Crow laws, and about an aunt who cannot tolerate piano music. Odetta's family moves to Los Angeles, and she is freed like a bird from everything that constricts her amazing talent. Told in free verse that could be song lyrics, the life of this woman, who influenced great musicians and rallied for noble causes, is recalled by an older generation and introduced to a younger one.

TEACHING IDEA

- Ask partners or small groups to select a contemporary song with appropriate lyrics for discussion. After students consider the rhythm and the style of the words to the song, they can write their own lyrics and share with the class. Remind students to pay attention to the sound of their lyrics, and to use alliteration and rich descriptive language.

INTERDISCIPLINARY CONNECTION

- Using the biographical information in the back of the book, instruct students to create a time line of the 1960s through the 1980s, noting important events and famous songs connected to those events.

The Remembering Stone

Written by Barbara Timberlake Russell
Illustrated by Claire B. Cotts
Farrar, Straus and Giroux, 2004, 32 pp.

In this book about personal and cultural identity, the importance of holding onto dreams is the central theme. Ana and her mother focus on returning to Costa Rica someday, and a rock from their homeland becomes a symbol for this desire. Ana's diverse friends and neighbors share their dreams and their ideas for making those dreams come true. The language of the story is lyrical and highlighted by Spanish vocabulary, which further supports the importance of cultural roots.

TEACHING IDEA

- Using *The Remembering Stone* as a model, invite students to bring in a special object from home that represents either a dream they have for the future or a symbol of their culture. Have students use a storyboard graphic organizer or invite them to share their dream, titling their project with the name they have chosen for the special object.

INTERDISCIPLINARY CONNECTION

■ Designate a day as "Coming to America" day, and ask students to bring in a story that they have collected from family about the history of how their family came to be in this country.

The Sea of Sleep

Written by Warren Hanson
Illustrated by Jim LaMarche
Scholastic Press, 2010, 32 pp.

This book tells the literal story of a mother and baby otter as they head out to sea for a good night's sleep in the way that otters do. The personified otters observe the beauty of the moon, and listen to the rhythm of the ocean in which they live. But figuratively speaking, this book rocks the reader to sleep using the ocean and otters as metaphors for the experience of falling into a deeply relaxing slumber. The language is lulling, and when you read it aloud, you find yourself rocked into a trance-like state by the repeating verses and dreamy imagery.

TEACHING IDEA

■ In small groups, invite students to consider various segments of their everyday school schedule, and ask them to prepare Readers Theater scripts from the personified point of view of an animal (e.g., a fly on the wall, a mouse looking out from a hole in the wall, a cat on a windowsill looking in).

INTERDISCIPLINARY CONNECTION

■ Encourage students to create, then play, a trivia game with information bits collected about unusual sleep habits of animals that students discover in research.

Sierra

Written by Diane Siebert
Illustrated by Wendell Mino
HarperCollins, 1991, 32 pp.

Sierra tells the story of the Sierra Nevada Mountains from the point of view of a mountain itself. A mountain is boldly personified, speaking in the first person, in rhyme, about its history and future. The mountain speaks of the creatures that inhabit the area and the challenges of survival. Repetition and rhyming couplets make the story of the seasonal changes, the plants and animals, and life cycle of the mountain an epic tale.

TEACHING IDEA

■ After reading *Sierra* aloud, provide students with a template for writing a nature poem in the style of Diane Siebert. Invite students to select an element of geography about which to write: "I am the _______ ." Encourage students to use rhyming couplets in their poem. When complete, publish poems in a class booklet or make time for a poetry slam to share work.

INTERDISCIPLINARY CONNECTION

■ Have students use photo presentation software to create a slide show of photos of the Sierra Nevada Mountains from images they find online. Use audio recording and editing software to record the voices of students reading the text of *Sierra* over the images of the mountains. Present the slide show to another class, or show it at a parent night.

Twilight Comes Twice

Written by Ralph Fletcher
Illustrated by Kate Kiesler
Clarion Books, 1997, 32 pp.

In this book, the special moments of dusk and dawn come to life as the author explains to the reader that both are described as twilight. The orangey glow of twilight comes twice a day as morning and night approach. At dusk, a young girl and family ready themselves for evening by enjoying the setting sun and creeping shadows of night. In the morning they are greeted by breakfast smells and daybreak. The images created by alliterative and mood-filled language fill us with magic that is complemented by the inviting artwork.

TEACHING IDEA

■ Provide pictures of landscape or cityscape paintings, by famous or not-so-famous artists, that can be found in library art books or online. Allow students to browse the paintings for one to use as inspiration. Ask students to write a free-verse poem that describes a very specific time of day that they see in the painting they have selected. Have them include at least three examples of figurative language in their poem. Use *Twilight Comes Twice* for inspiration and example.

INTERDISCIPLINARY CONNECTION

■ The animal and insect life that is spurred into action at dusk has some unique qualities. Mosquitoes, bats, and fireflies each contribute to the twilight experience in good and bad ways. Ask students to explore and report on one interesting aspect of twilight animal life.

Where the Sunrise Begins

Written by Douglas Wood
Illustrated by Wendy Popp
Simon & Schuster Books for Young Readers, 2010, 40 pp.

Beginning by asking the question, "Where does the sunrise begin?" the author sets up a repeating pattern that draws the reader in with a wide range of moving figurative language. Each response to the question starts with "Some say it begins . . . ." Readers are taken on a journey in search of the beginning sunrise, traveling to many different geographical regions, each having its own claim to fame. Ultimately readers learn that "every moment brings the sunrise to someone" and that the sunrise is within each of us. In this way, sunrise becomes a metaphor for hope and the fresh start of each new day.

TEACHING IDEA

■ Ask students to brainstorm a list of scientific concepts that could be used as a metaphor for an abstract concept by using the analogy: *Sunrise is to hope as ______ is to ______*. Provide an opportunity for students to share in small groups, revise, and rewrite, and select an analogy around which to build a group story.

INTERDISCIPLINARY CONNECTION

■ Offer students an opportunity to investigate sunrise as an astronomical event. There are videos available online that show Earth at sunrise from space at sunrise, as well as animated versions of daybreak. Create a class video or slide show of a sunrise collage that might include live shots of dawn, or possibly a video of the students creating their own scientific demonstration using flashlights and basketballs held to represent the earth and sun.

SIMILE PORTRAIT MODEL

Pop Pop

I adore my grandpa.

I call him Pop Pop.

He is as old as the Rocky Mountains.

His hair is the color of Christmas tree tinsel,

And his face is as creased as parchment.

He wears a flannel shirt

As soft as the wool of a newborn lamb.

When he works, he moves

Like a playful bull calf.

About me, my Pop Pop says,

"You are my sugar plum."

SIMILE PORTRAIT

Name: ______________________________

____
(title)

I adore my ______________________________.
(relative's name)

I call ____________ ______________________________.
(him/her) (nickname)

____________ is as old as ______________________,
(He/She)

And ____________ face is as ____________________ as ______________________.
(his/her) (simile)

____________ wears a ______________________________
(He/She)

As ____________________ as ______________________________.
(simile)

When __________ works, __________ moves
(he/she) (he/she)

Like ______________________________.
(simile for how he/she moves)

About me, my ______________________________ says,
(relative's name)

"______________________________."

HYPERBOLE AND CARICATURES

Name: ____________________

As you listen to your teacher read the descriptions of *Backward Bart*, record the hyperboles in the appropriate area of the graphic organizer. After collecting the hyperboles, work with a partner to analyze the effect the hyperbole has on your understanding of Bart's character.

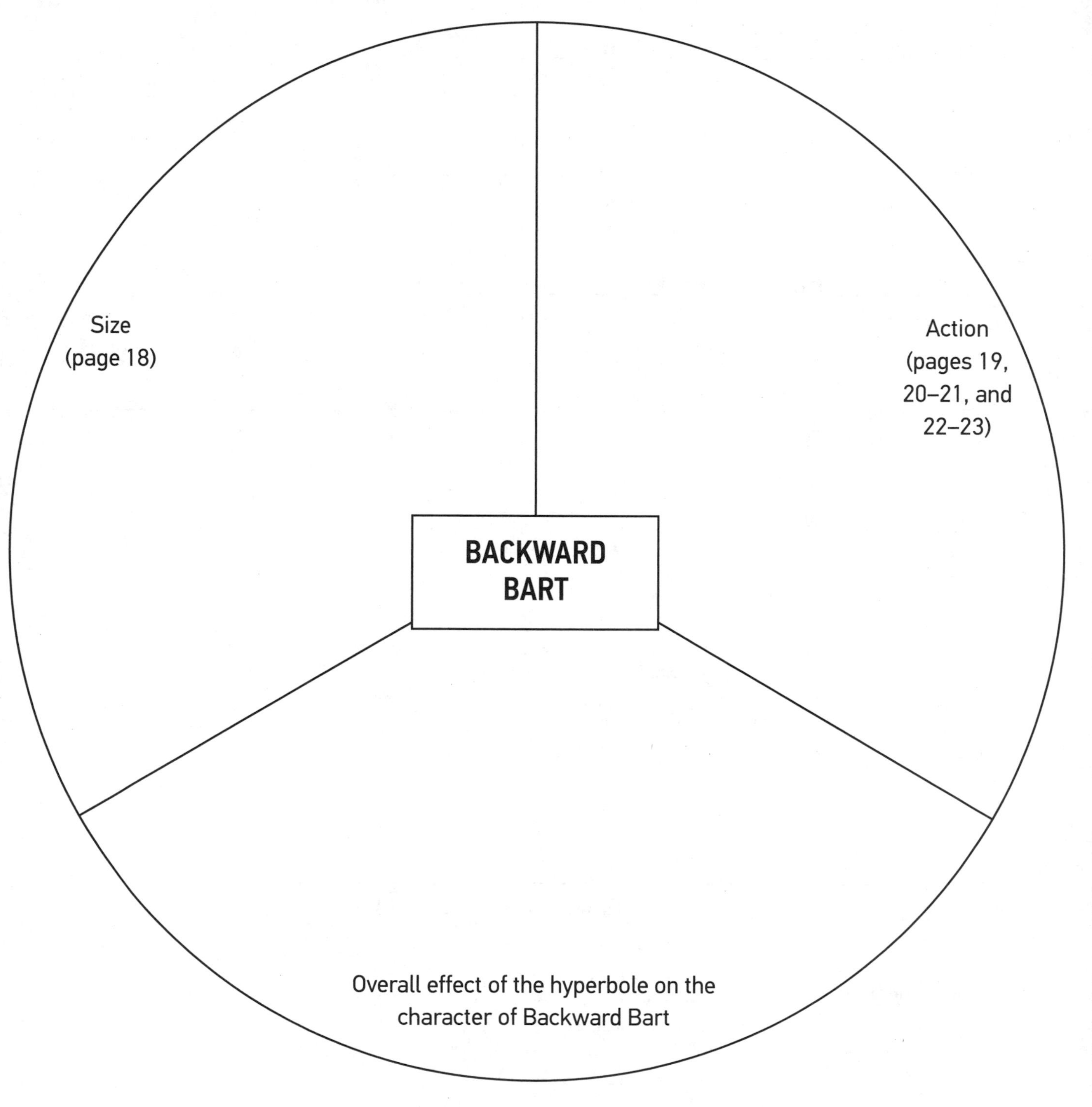

A HYPERBOLE PORTRAIT

In the picture frame below, create a caricature of yourself and super-size your physical features. Then create three hyperboles that exaggerate admirable qualities friends and family have recognized in you.

HYPERBOLES ABOUT ME

1. ____

____

2. ____

____

3. ____

____

REFERENCES

Frayer, D., Frederick, W. C., & Klausmeier, H. J. (1969). *A schema for testing the level of cognitive mastery*. Madison, WI: Wisconsin Center for Education Research.

Hall, S. (2002). *Using picture storybooks to teach literary devices* (Volume 3). Westport: Oryx Press.

Harste, J. C., Short, K. G., & Burke, C. (1988). *Creating classrooms for authors: The reading-writing connection*. Portsmouth, NH: Heinemann.

Kane, S. (2008*). Integrating literature in the content areas: Enhancing adolescent learning and literacy*. Scottsdale, AZ: Holcomb Hathaway Publishers.

Langer, J. (2011). *Envisioning literature: Literary understanding and literature instruction*. New York: Teachers College Press.

Lukens, R. (2006). *A critical handbook of children's literature,* 7th ed. New York: Allyn and Bacon.

McLaughlin, M., & Allen, M. B. (2002). *Guided comprehension: A teaching model for grades 3–8*. Newark, DE: International Reading Association.

Moss, B. (2005). Making a case and a place for effective content area literacy instruction in the elementary grades. *The Reading Teacher*, *59*(1), 46–55.

Olness, R. (2005). *Using literature to enhance writing instruction*. Newark: International Reading Association.

Roberts, S. K. (2009). Navigating the normal chaos of middle school: Using poetry to promote peaceful classrooms. *Focus on Middle School Quarterly*, *21*(4), 1–5.

Santa, C. M. (1988). *Content reading including study systems: Reading, writing, and studying across the curriculum*. Dubuque, IA: Kendall/Hunt Pub. Co.

Serafini, F. (2009). Understanding visual images in picturebooks. In J. Evans (Ed.,) *Talking beyond the page: Reading and responding to contemporary picturebooks*. London: Routledge.

Smith, M. W., & Wilhelm, J. D. (2010). *Fresh takes on teaching literary elements: How to teach what really matters about character, setting, point of view, and theme*. New York: Scholastic.

Tompkins, G. (2001). *Literacy for the 21st century: A balanced approach* (2nd ed.). New York: Prentice Hall.

Van Zile, S., & Napoli, M. (2009). *Teaching literary elements with picture books*. New York: Scholastic.

Vásquez, A. (2009). Breathing underwater: At-risk ninth graders dive into literary analysis. *The ALAN Review*, *37*(1), 1–16.

AUTHOR INDEX

TITLE INDEX